MUSICAL INTERLUDE

CHAPTER ONE

WRITTEN BY
SHAWN GABBORIN

ART BY
RAFAEL DANTAS

COLORS BY
ROSA "ROSAKAZ" RANTILA

SPECIAL THANKS TO DANIEL J. LOGAN

COVERS A & B
ZOE STANLEY

COVERS C & D
TREVOR GRACE

COVERS E & F
WINSTON YOUNG

Jason Martin: Publisher
Shawn Gabborin: Editor in Chief
Nicole D'Andria: Marketing Director/Editor
Danielle Davison: Executive Administrator
Bryan Seaton: CEO
Shawn Pryor: President of Creator Relations

BLACK BETTY #5 . June 2018. Copyright Shawn Gabborin and Action Lab Entertainment, Inc. 2018. Published by Action Lab Comics. All rights reserved. All characters are fictional. Any likeness to anyone living or dead is purely coincidental. No part of this publication may be reproduced or transmitted without permission, except for small excerpts for review purposes. Printed in Canada. First printing. Actionlabcomics.com

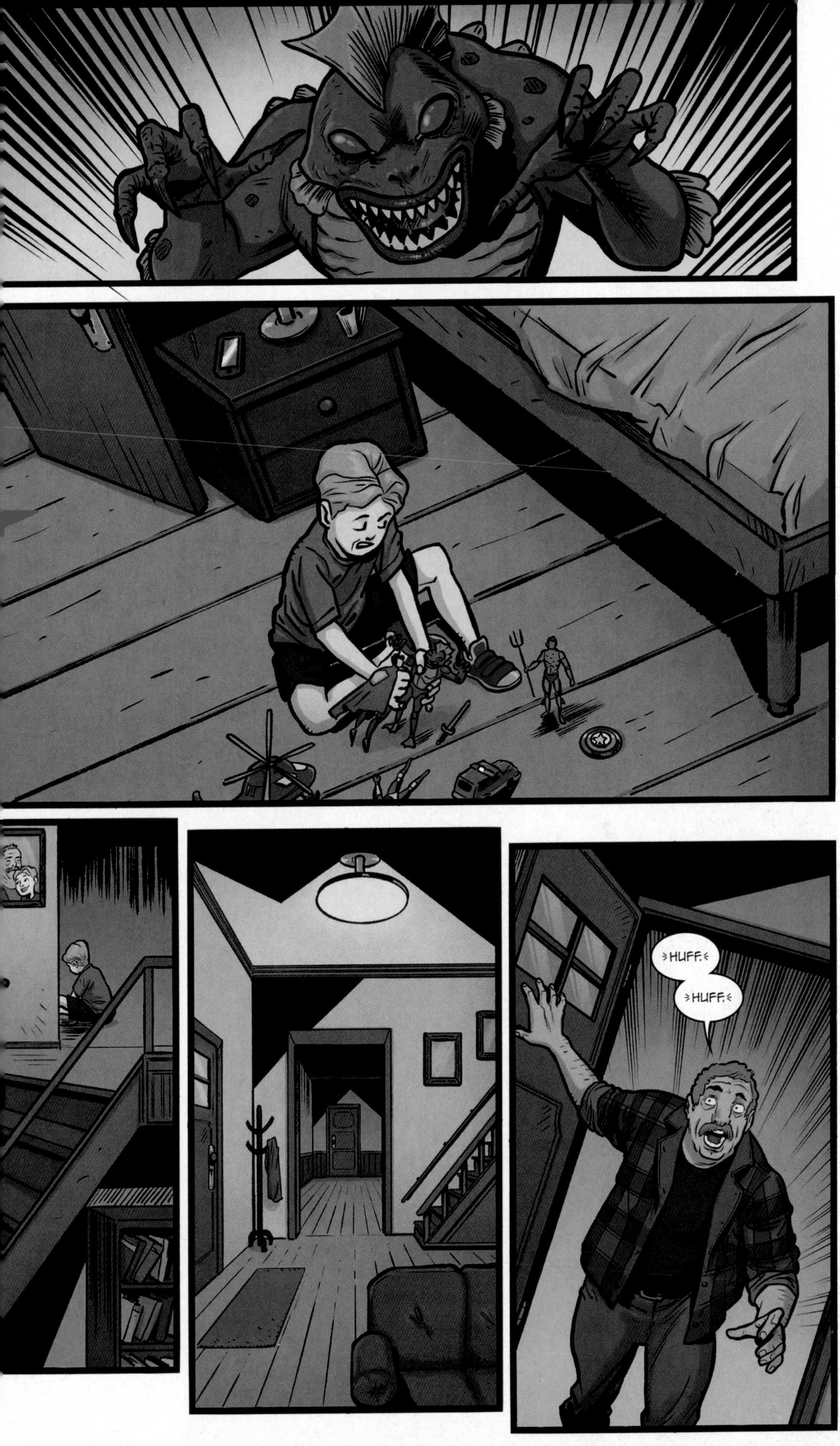
HUFF
HUFF

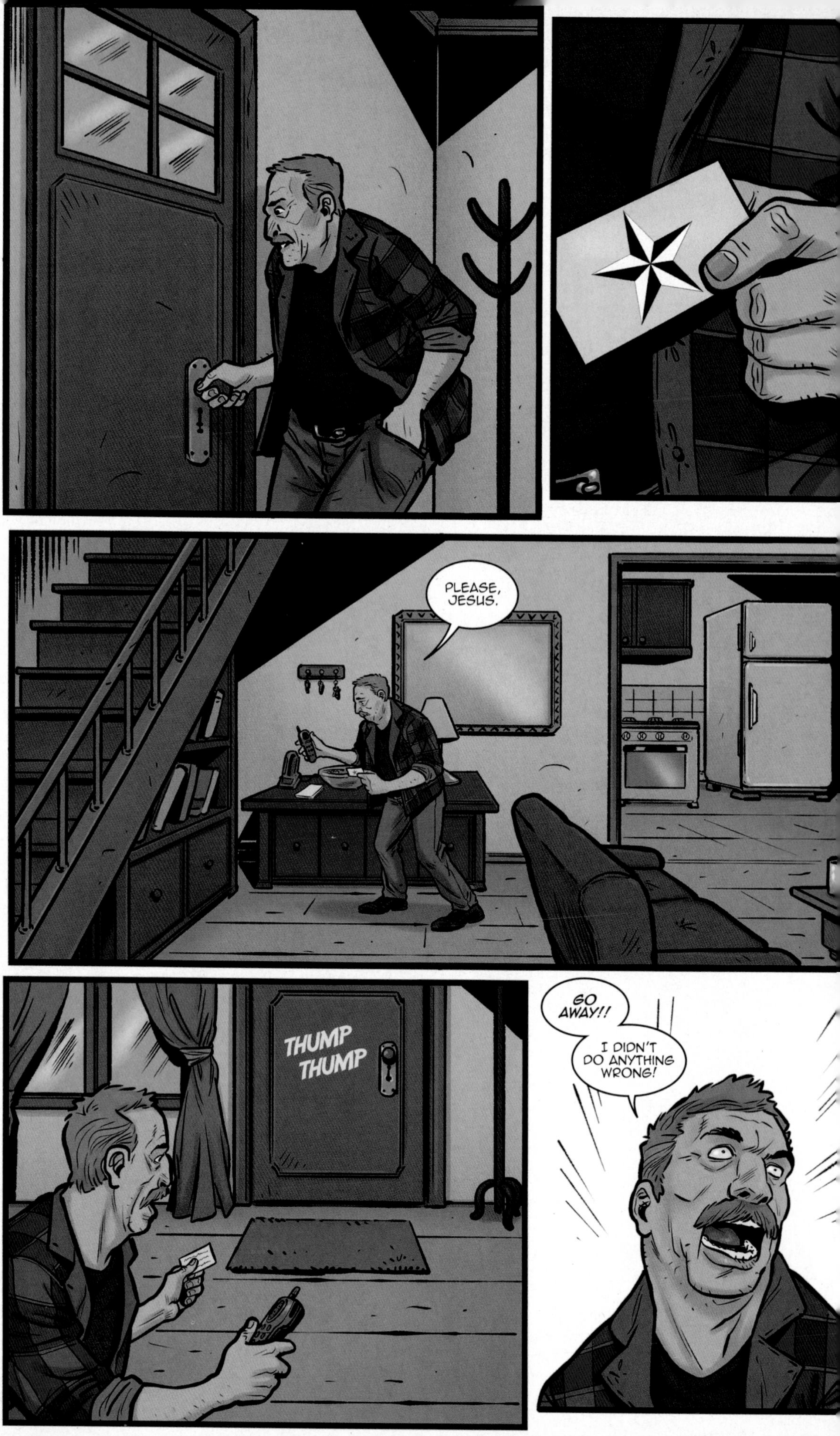
PLEASE, JESUS.
THUMP THUMP
GO AWAY!!
I DIDN'T DO ANYTHING WRONG!

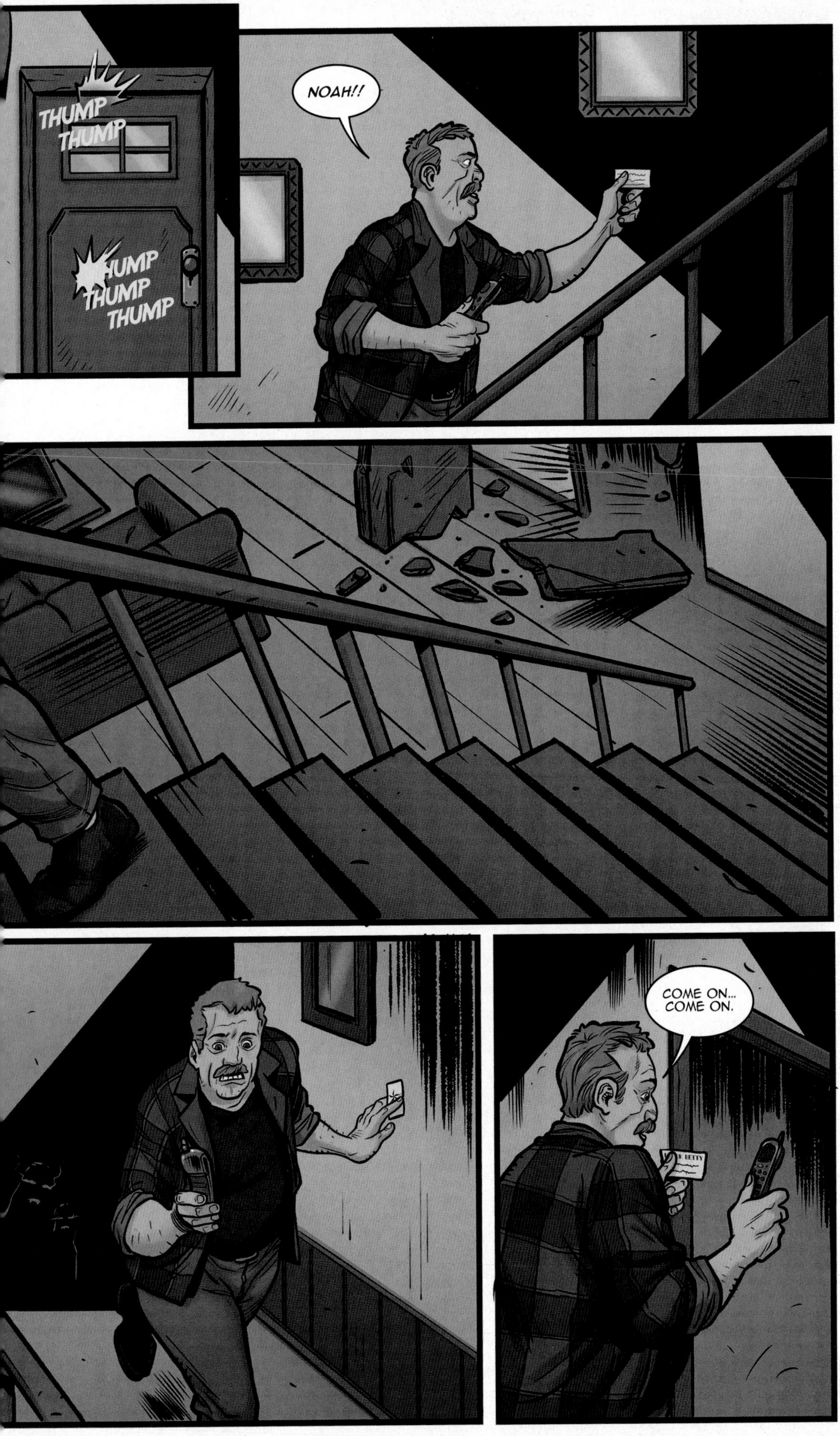
THUMP
THUMP
THUMP
THUMP
THUMP
NOAH!!
COME ON... COME ON.

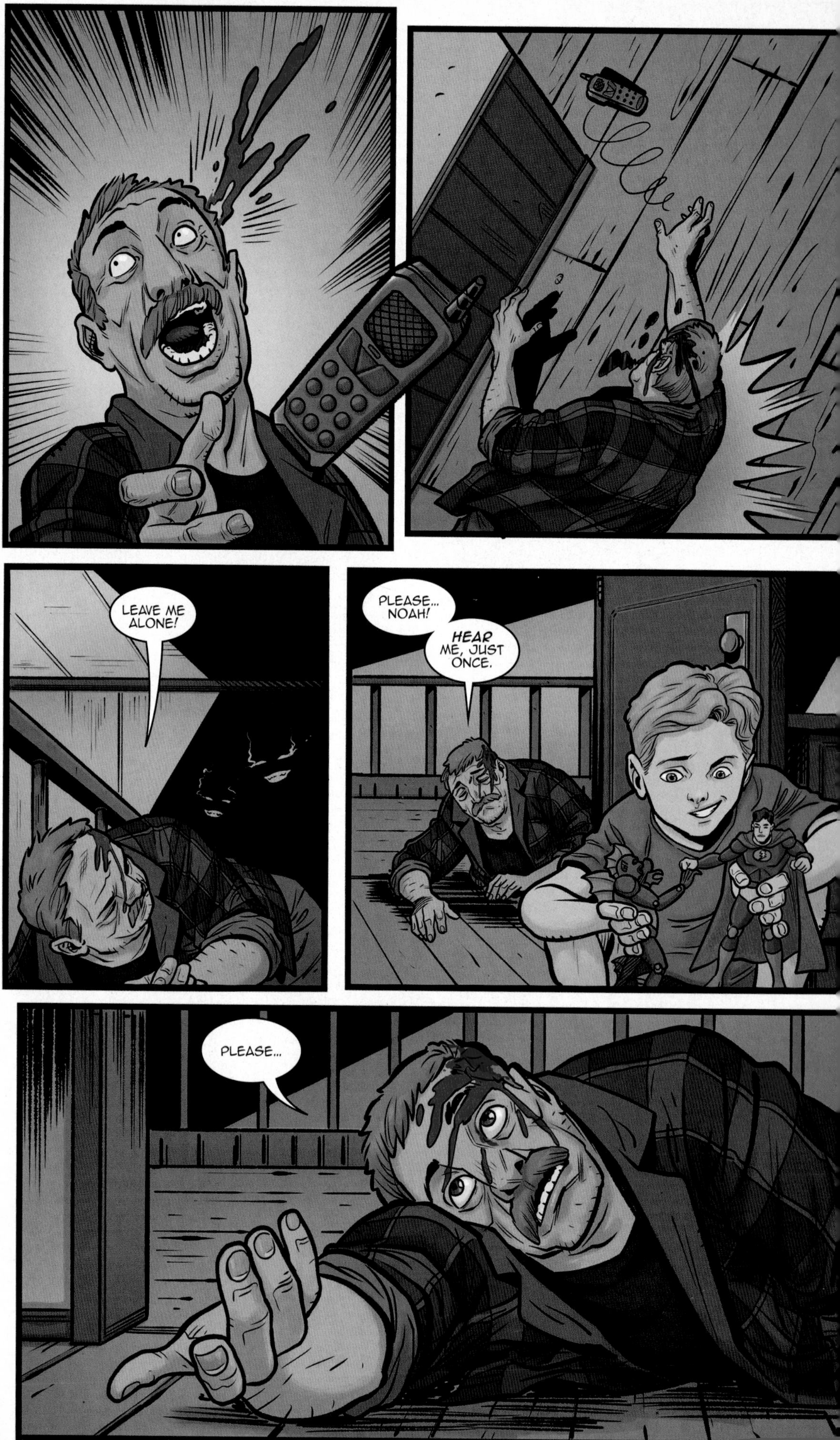
LEAVE ME ALONE!
PLEASE... NOAH!
HEAR ME, JUST ONCE.
PLEASE...

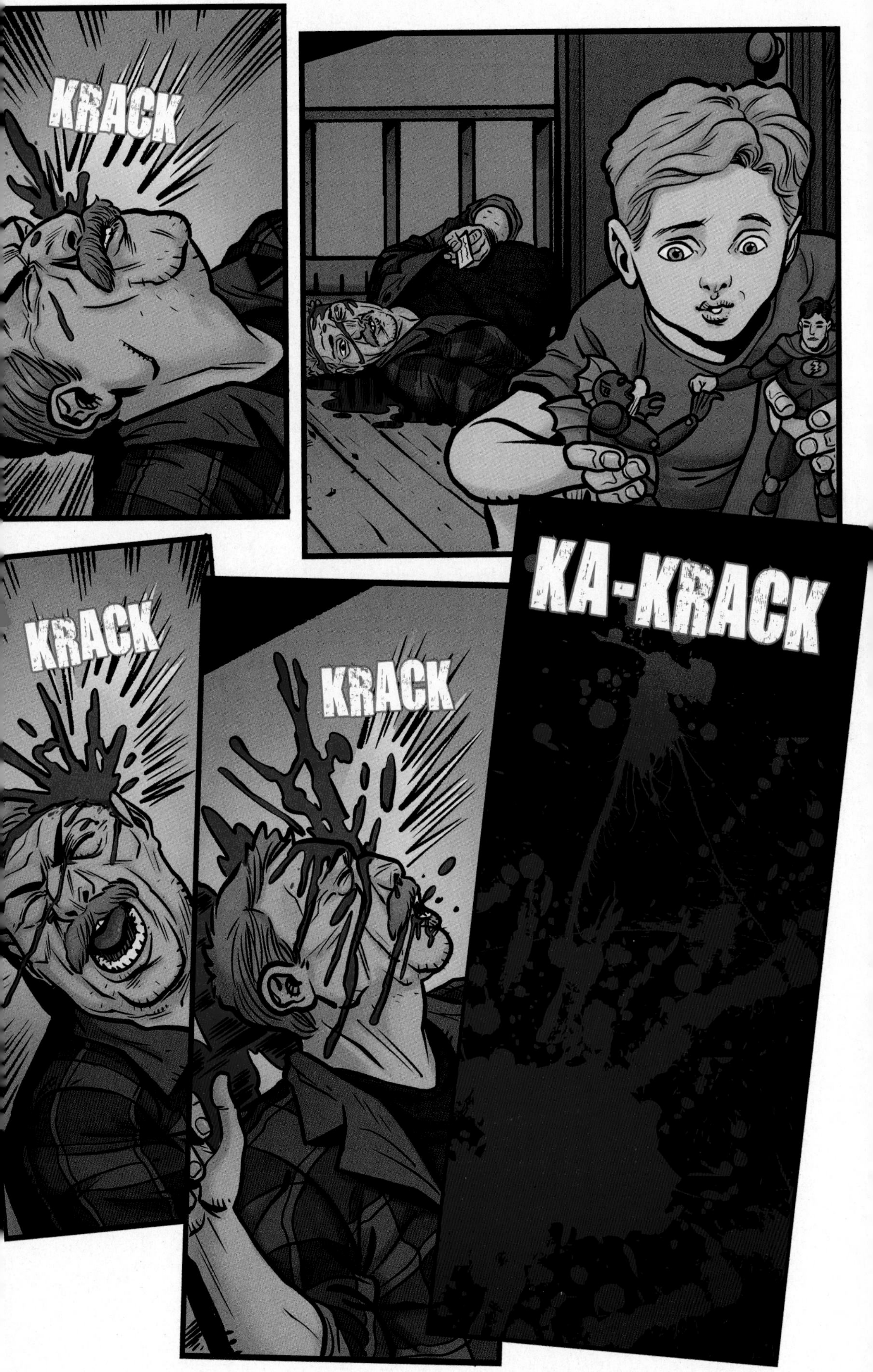
KRACK
KRACK
KRACK
KA-KRACK

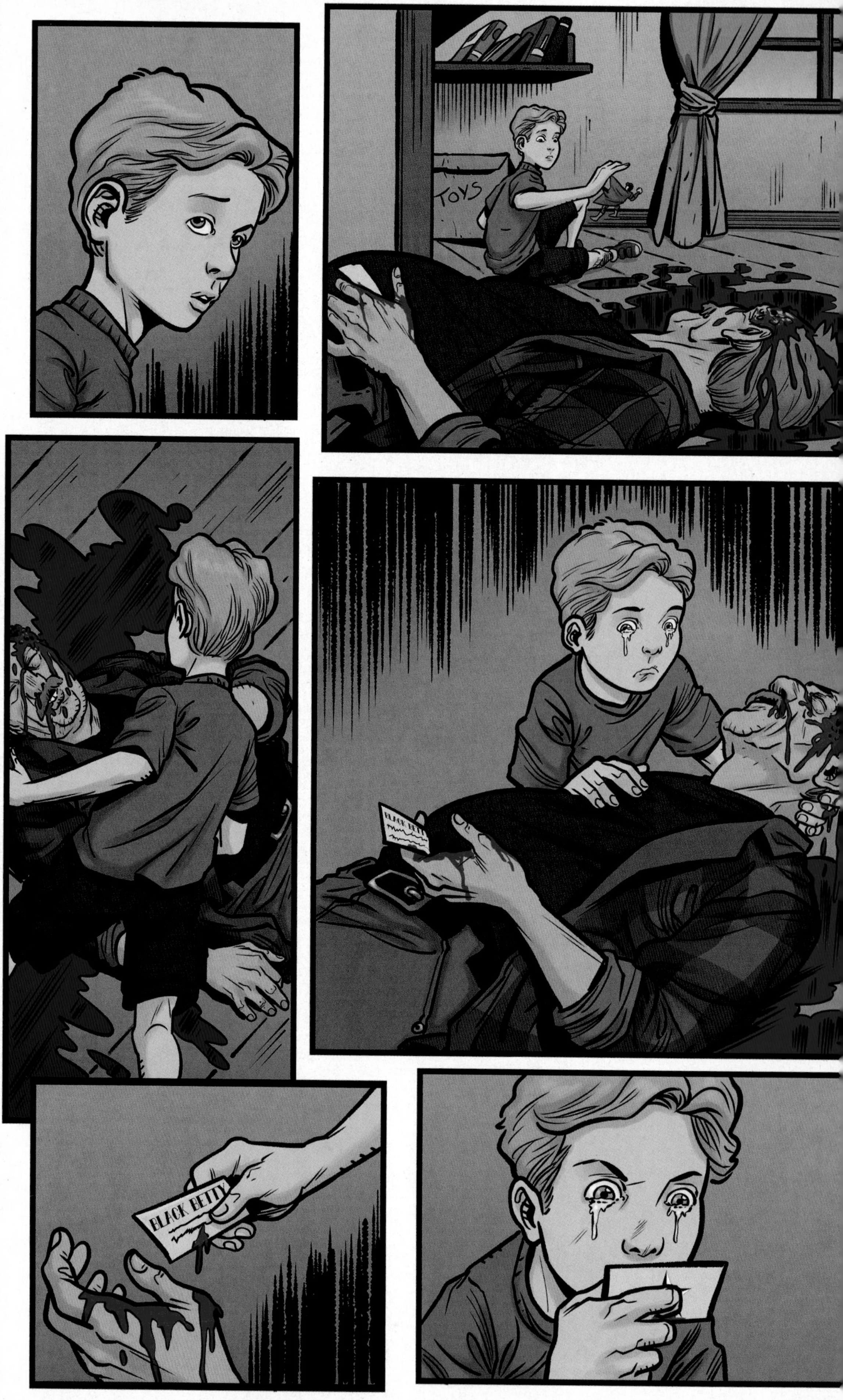
TOYS
BLACK BETTY

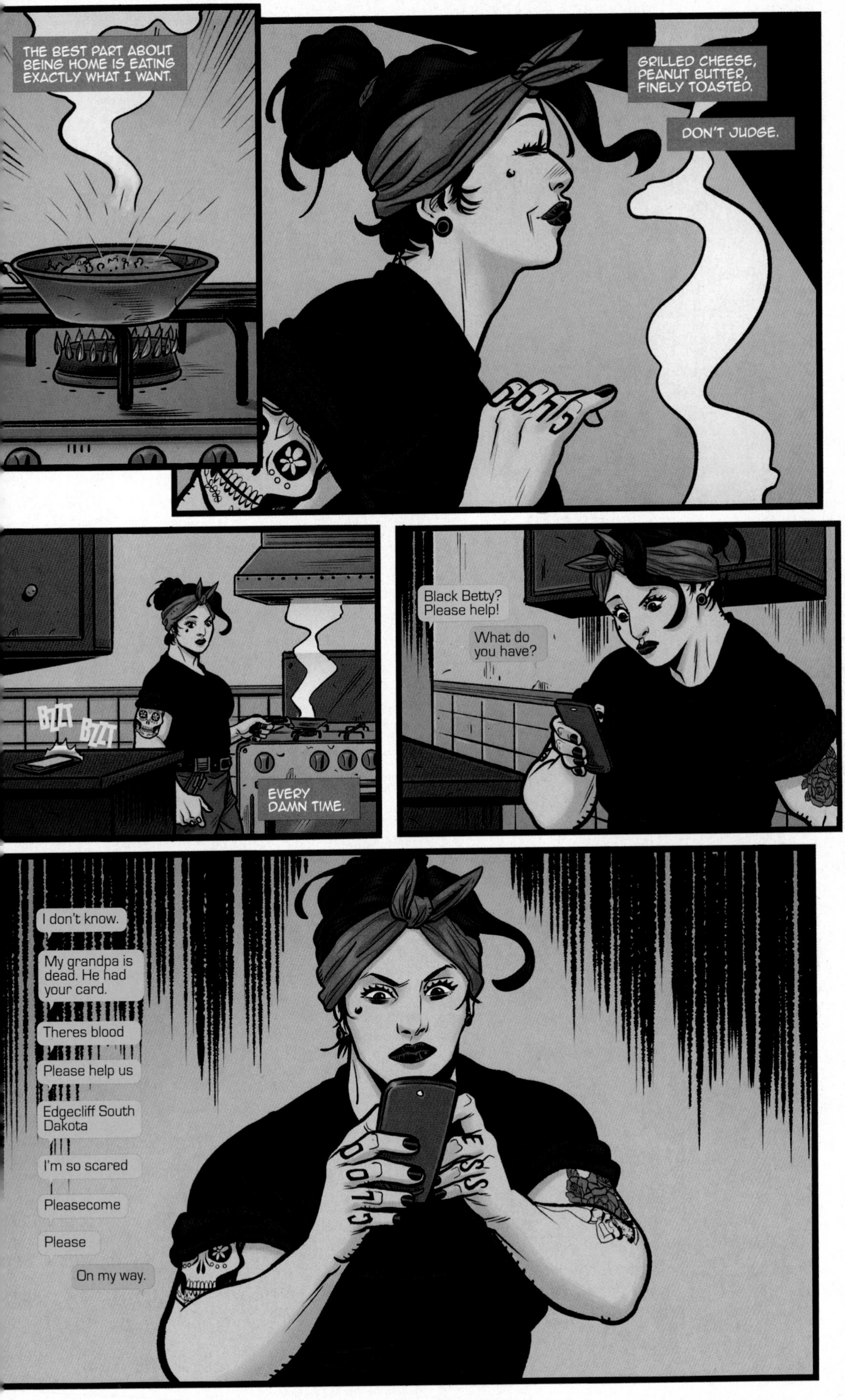
THE BEST PART ABOUT BEING HOME IS EATING EXACTLY WHAT I WANT.
GRILLED CHEESE, PEANUT BUTTER, FINELY TOASTED.
DON'T JUDGE.
BZZT BZZT
EVERY DAMN TIME.
Black Betty? Please help!
What do you have?
I don't know.
My grandpa is dead. He had your card.
Theres blood
Please help us
Edgecliff South Dakota
I'm so scared
Pleasecome
Please
On my way.

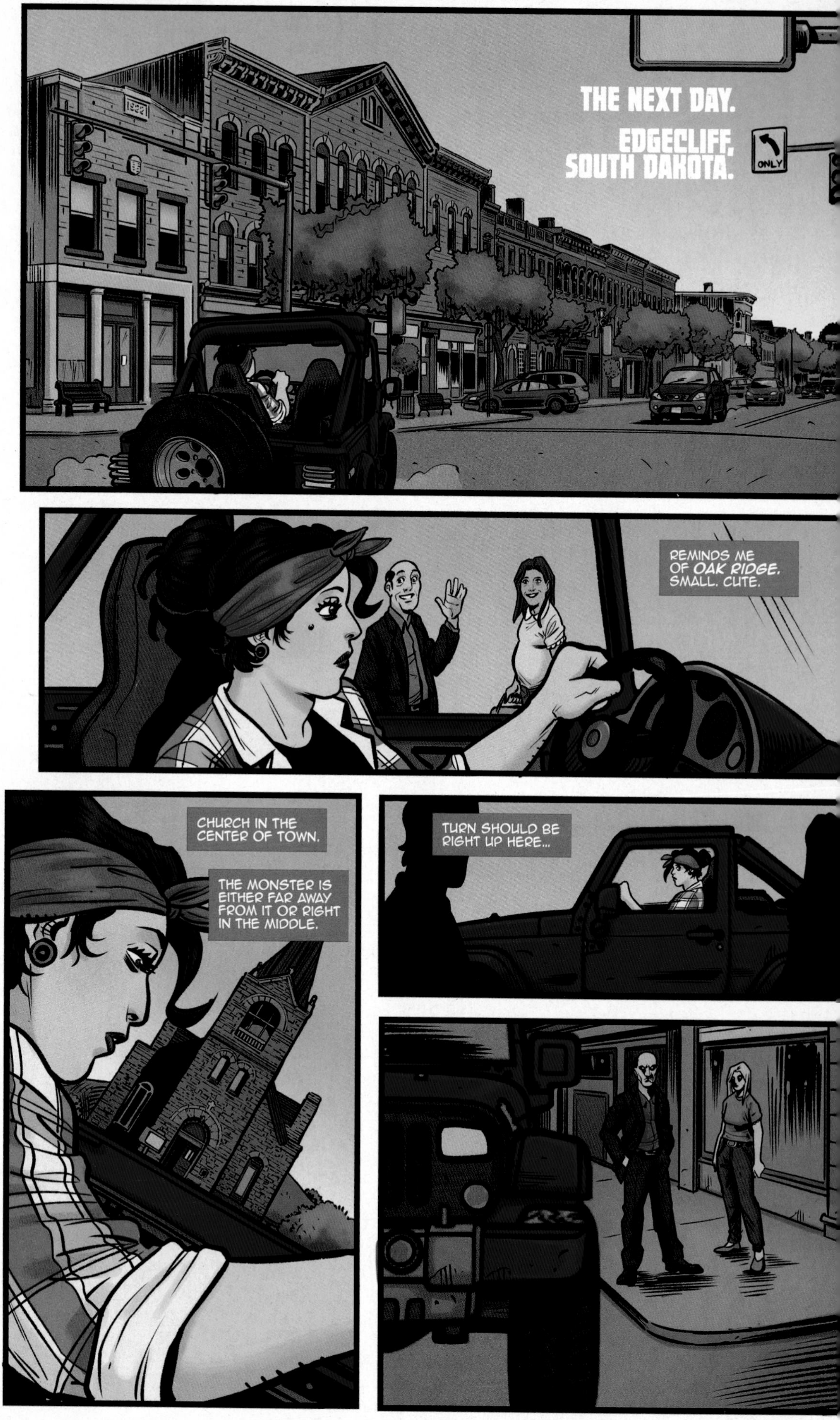
THE NEXT DAY.
EDGECLIFF, SOUTH DAKOTA.
ONLY
REMINDS ME OF OAK RIDGE. SMALL. CUTE.
CHURCH IN THE CENTER OF TOWN.
THE MONSTER IS EITHER FAR AWAY FROM IT OR RIGHT IN THE MIDDLE.
TURN SHOULD BE RIGHT UP HERE...

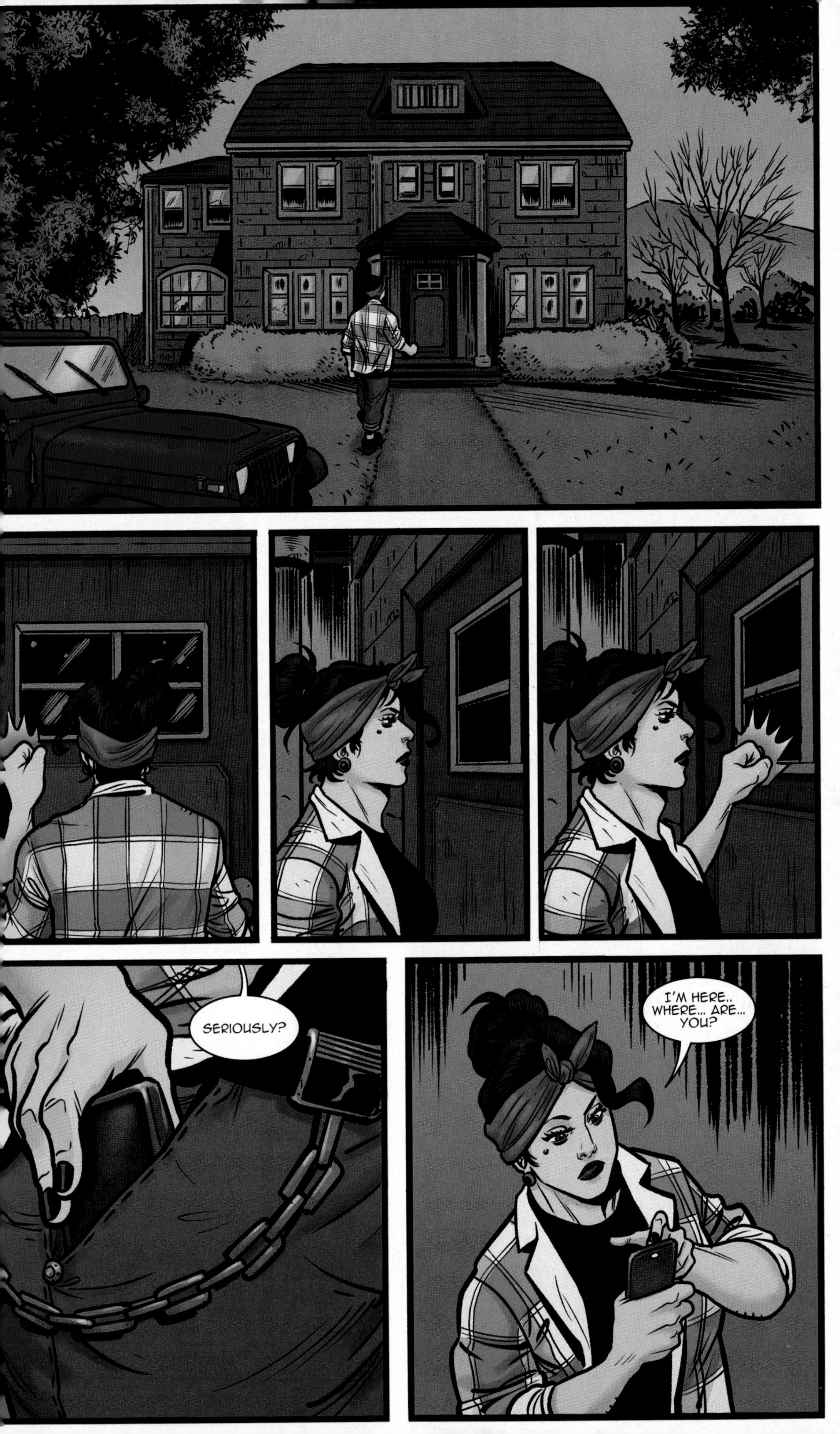
SERIOUSLY?
I'M HERE.. WHERE... ARE... YOU?

HEY, THERE. YOU NOAH?

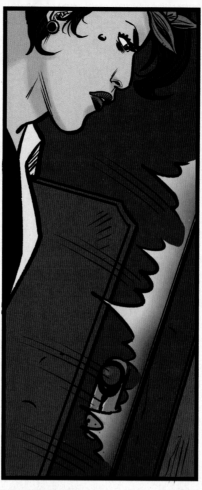

LOOK, KID. I TOOK A CHANCE ANSWERING YOUR TEXTS... BUT I'M NOT HERE TO PLAY.

I'M NOT TRYING TO SCOLD YOU OR ANYTHING. I JUST NEED TO KNOW WHAT'S WHAT, OKAY?

SO YOU'RE NOT EVEN GOING TO ANSWER?

"I'M DEAF"

WELL, THAT EXPLAINS SOME THINGS.

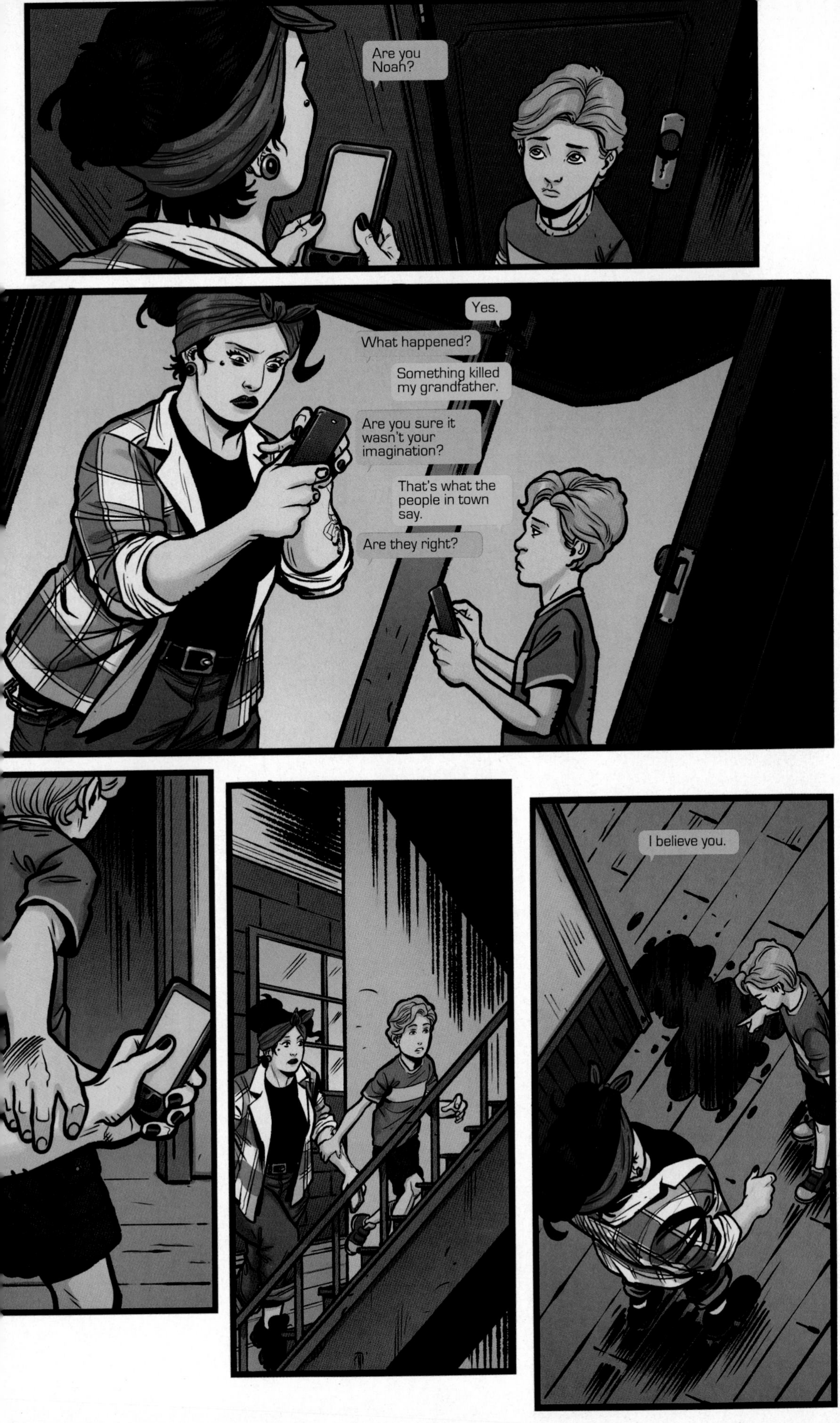
Are you Noah?
Yes.
What happened?
Something killed my grandfather.
Are you sure it wasn't your imagination?
That's what the people in town say.
Are they right?
I believe you.

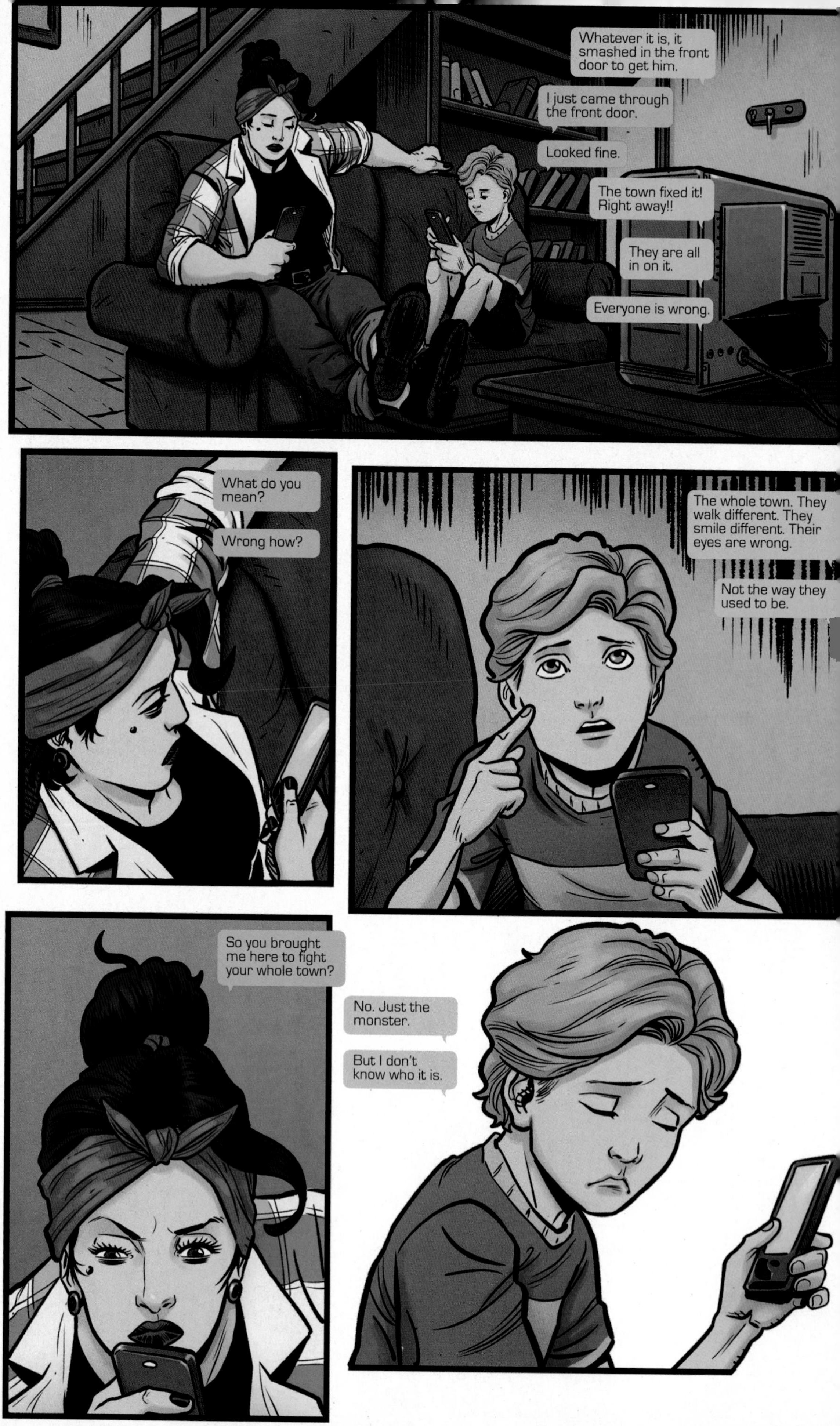
Whatever it is, it smashed in the front door to get him.
I just came through the front door.
Looked fine.
The town fixed it! Right away!!
They are all in on it.
Everyone is wrong.
What do you mean?
Wrong how?
The whole town. They walk different. They smile different. Their eyes are wrong.
Not the way they used to be.
So you brought me here to fight your whole town?
No. Just the monster.
But I don't know who it is.

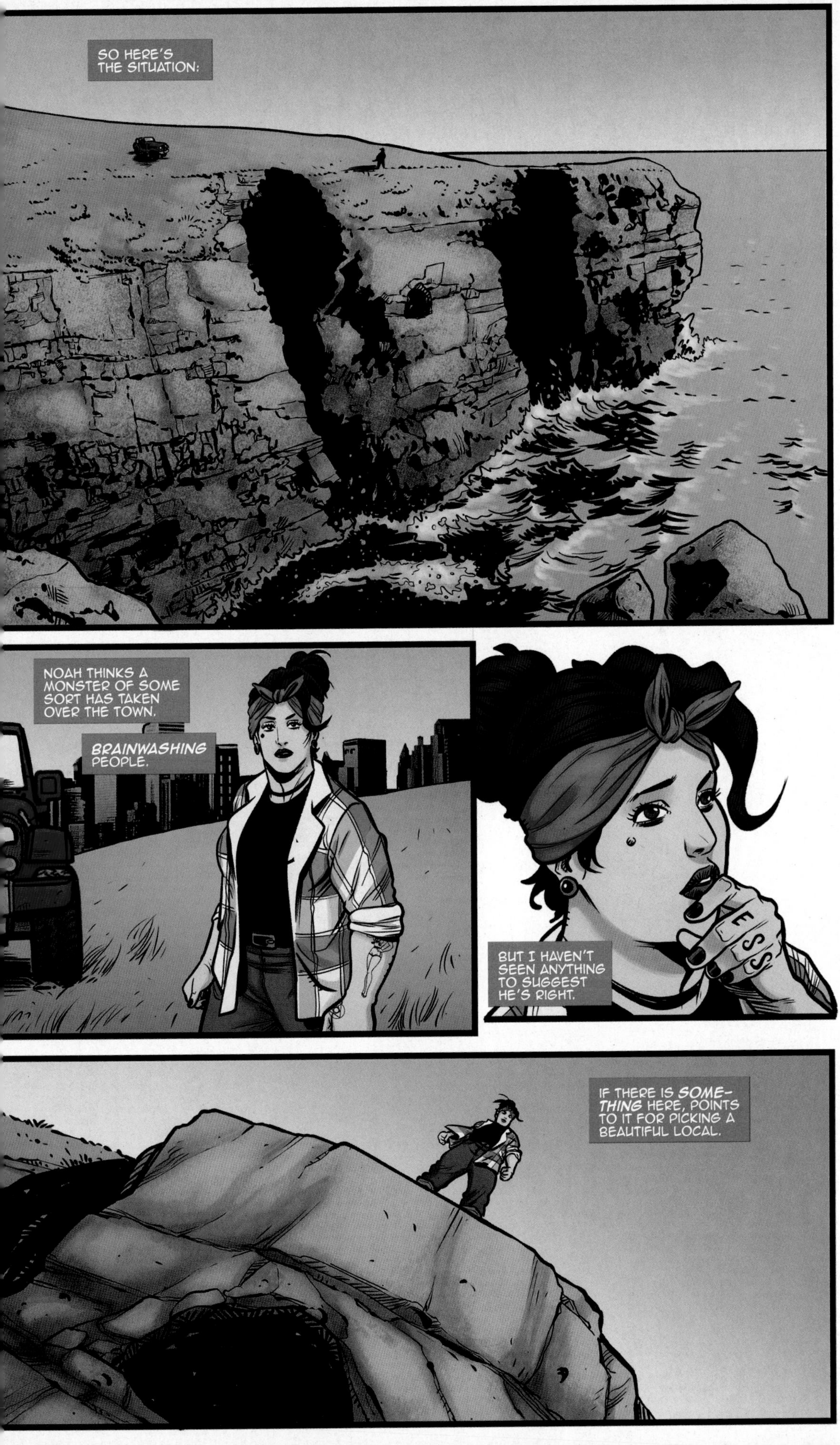
SO HERE'S THE SITUATION:
NOAH THINKS A MONSTER OF SOME SORT HAS TAKEN OVER THE TOWN.
BRAINWASHING PEOPLE.
BUT I HAVEN'T SEEN ANYTHING TO SUGGEST HE'S RIGHT.
IF THERE IS SOMETHING HERE, POINTS TO IT FOR PICKING A BEAUTIFUL LOCAL.

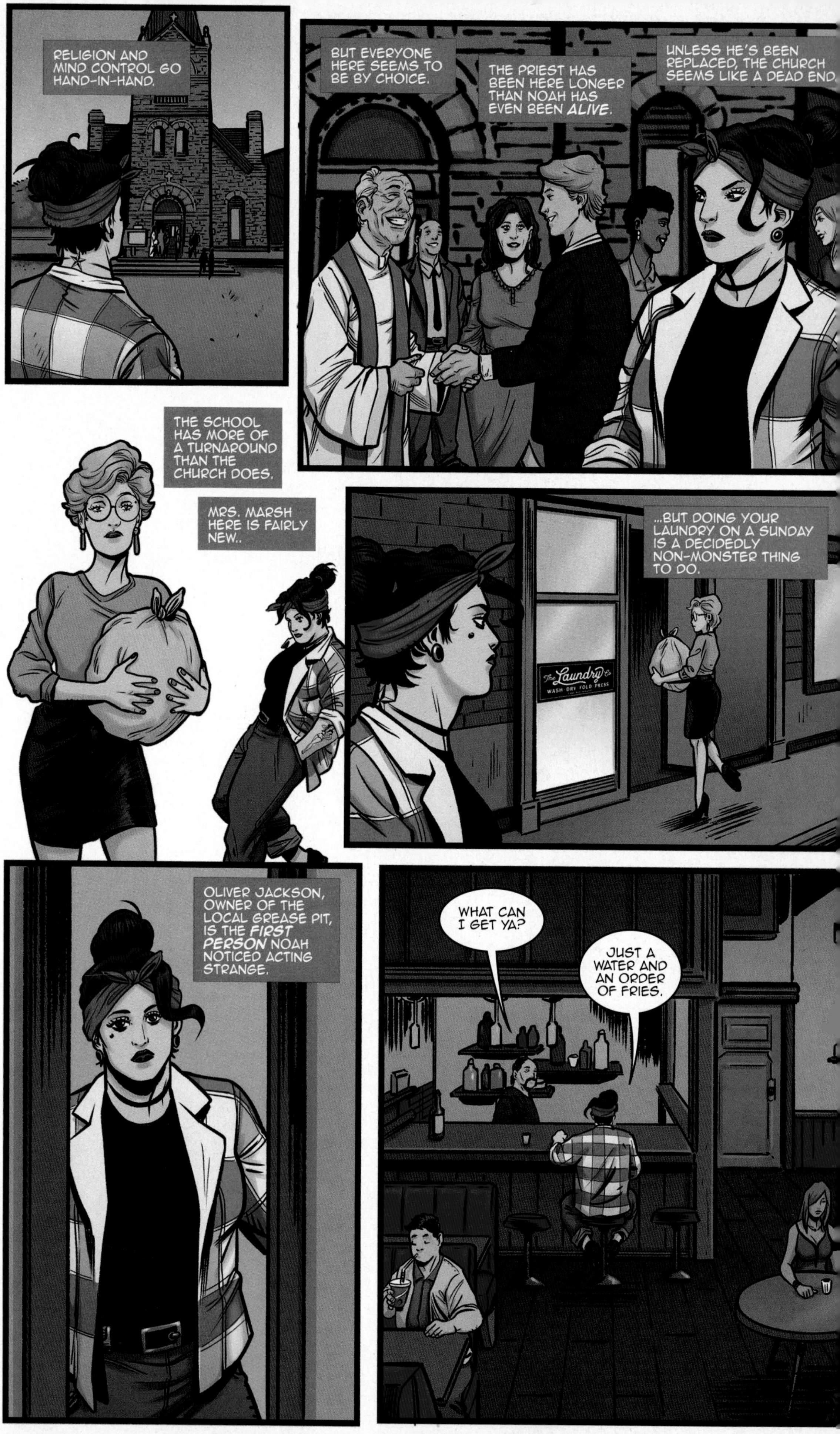
RELIGION AND MIND CONTROL GO HAND-IN-HAND.
BUT EVERYONE HERE SEEMS TO BE BY CHOICE.
THE PRIEST HAS BEEN HERE LONGER THAN NOAH HAS EVEN BEEN *ALIVE*.
UNLESS HE'S BEEN REPLACED, THE CHURCH SEEMS LIKE A DEAD END.
THE SCHOOL HAS MORE OF A TURNAROUND THAN THE CHURCH DOES.
MRS. MARSH HERE IS FAIRLY NEW..
...BUT DOING YOUR LAUNDRY ON A SUNDAY IS A DECIDEDLY NON-MONSTER THING TO DO.
The Laundry Co.
WASH · DRY · FOLD · PRESS
OLIVER JACKSON, OWNER OF THE LOCAL GREASE PIT, IS THE *FIRST PERSON* NOAH NOTICED ACTING STRANGE.
WHAT CAN I GET YA?
JUST A WATER AND AN ORDER OF FRIES.

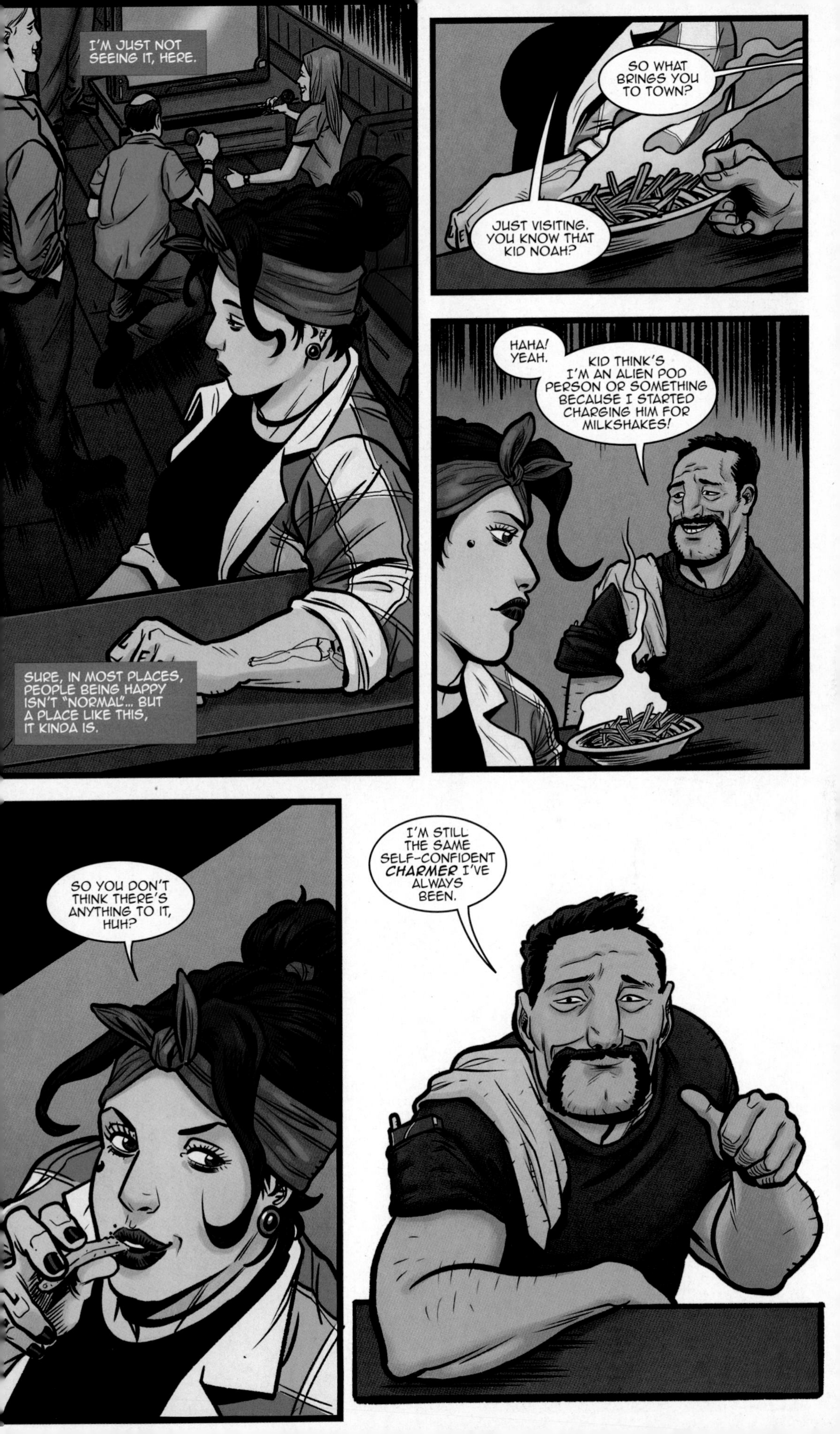
I'M JUST NOT SEEING IT, HERE.
SURE, IN MOST PLACES, PEOPLE BEING HAPPY ISN'T "NORMAL"... BUT A PLACE LIKE THIS, IT KINDA IS.
SO WHAT BRINGS YOU TO TOWN?
JUST VISITING. YOU KNOW THAT KID NOAH?
HAHA! YEAH.
KID THINK'S I'M AN ALIEN POD PERSON OR SOMETHING BECAUSE I STARTED CHARGING HIM FOR MILKSHAKES!
SO YOU DON'T THINK THERE'S ANYTHING TO IT, HUH?
I'M STILL THE SAME SELF-CONFIDENT *CHARMER* I'VE ALWAYS BEEN.

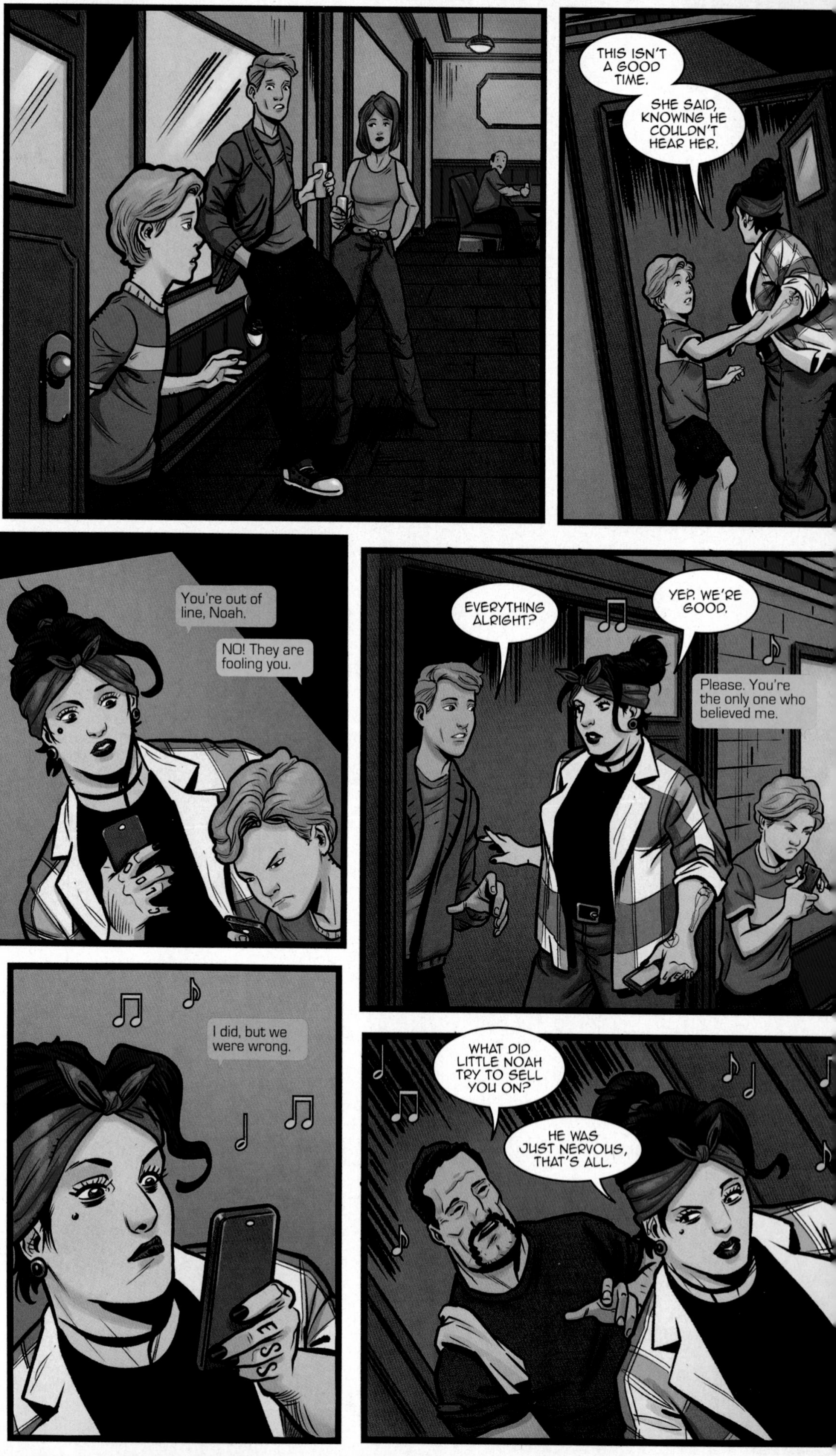
THIS ISN'T A GOOD TIME.
SHE SAID, KNOWING HE COULDN'T HEAR HER.
You're out of line, Noah.
NO! They are fooling you.
EVERYTHING ALRIGHT?
YEP. WE'RE GOOD.
Please. You're the only one who believed me.
I did, but we were wrong.
WHAT DID LITTLE NOAH TRY TO SELL YOU ON?
HE WAS JUST NERVOUS, THAT'S ALL.

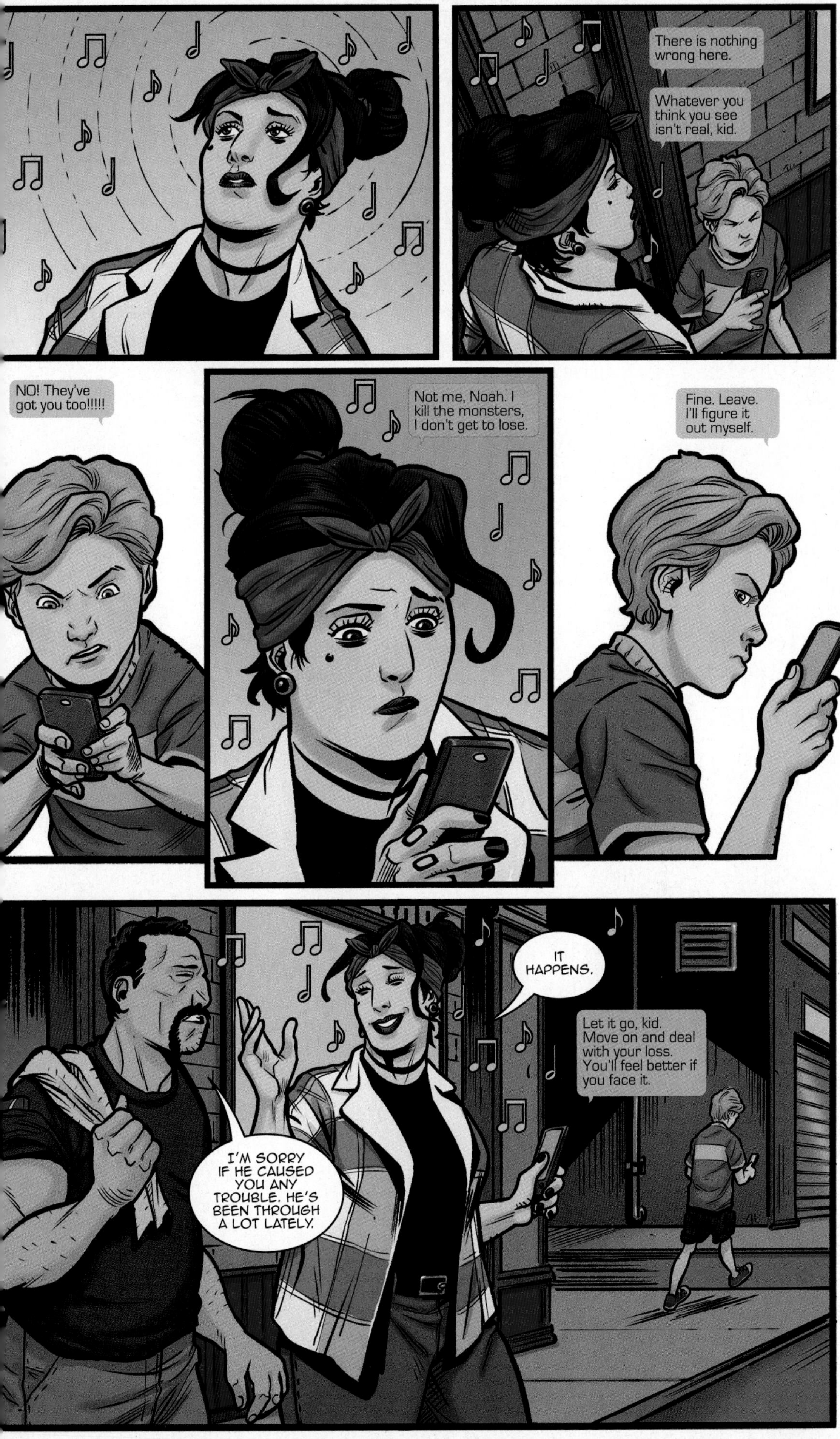

There is nothing wrong here.
Whatever you think you see isn't real, kid.
NO! They've got you too!!!!!
Not me, Noah. I kill the monsters, I don't get to lose.
Fine. Leave. I'll figure it out myself.
I'M SORRY IF HE CAUSED YOU ANY TROUBLE. HE'S BEEN THROUGH A LOT LATELY.
IT HAPPENS.
Let it go, kid. Move on and deal with your loss. You'll feel better if you face it.

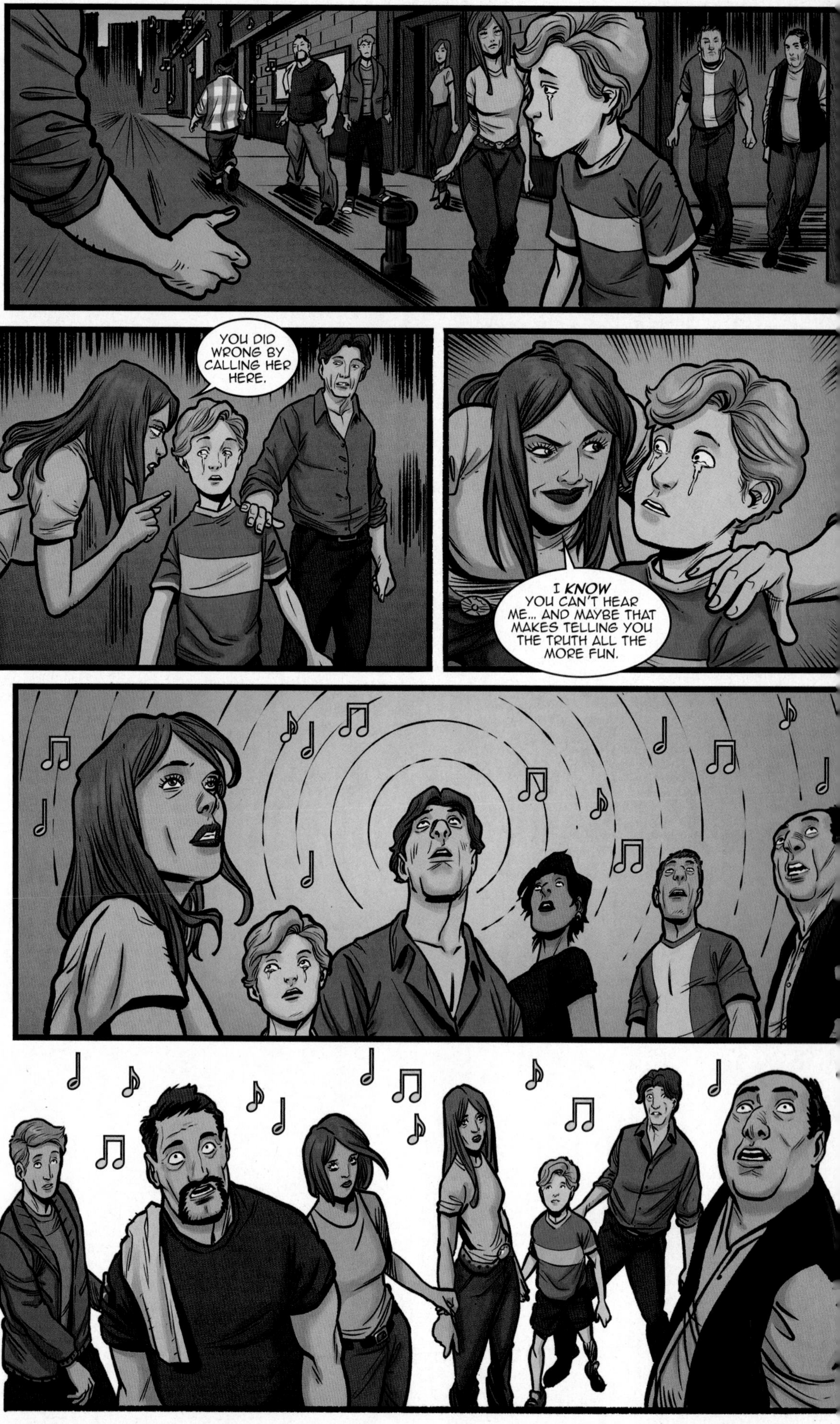
YOU DID WRONG BY CALLING HER HERE.
I *KNOW* YOU CAN'T HEAR ME... AND MAYBE THAT MAKES TELLING YOU THE TRUTH ALL THE MORE FUN.

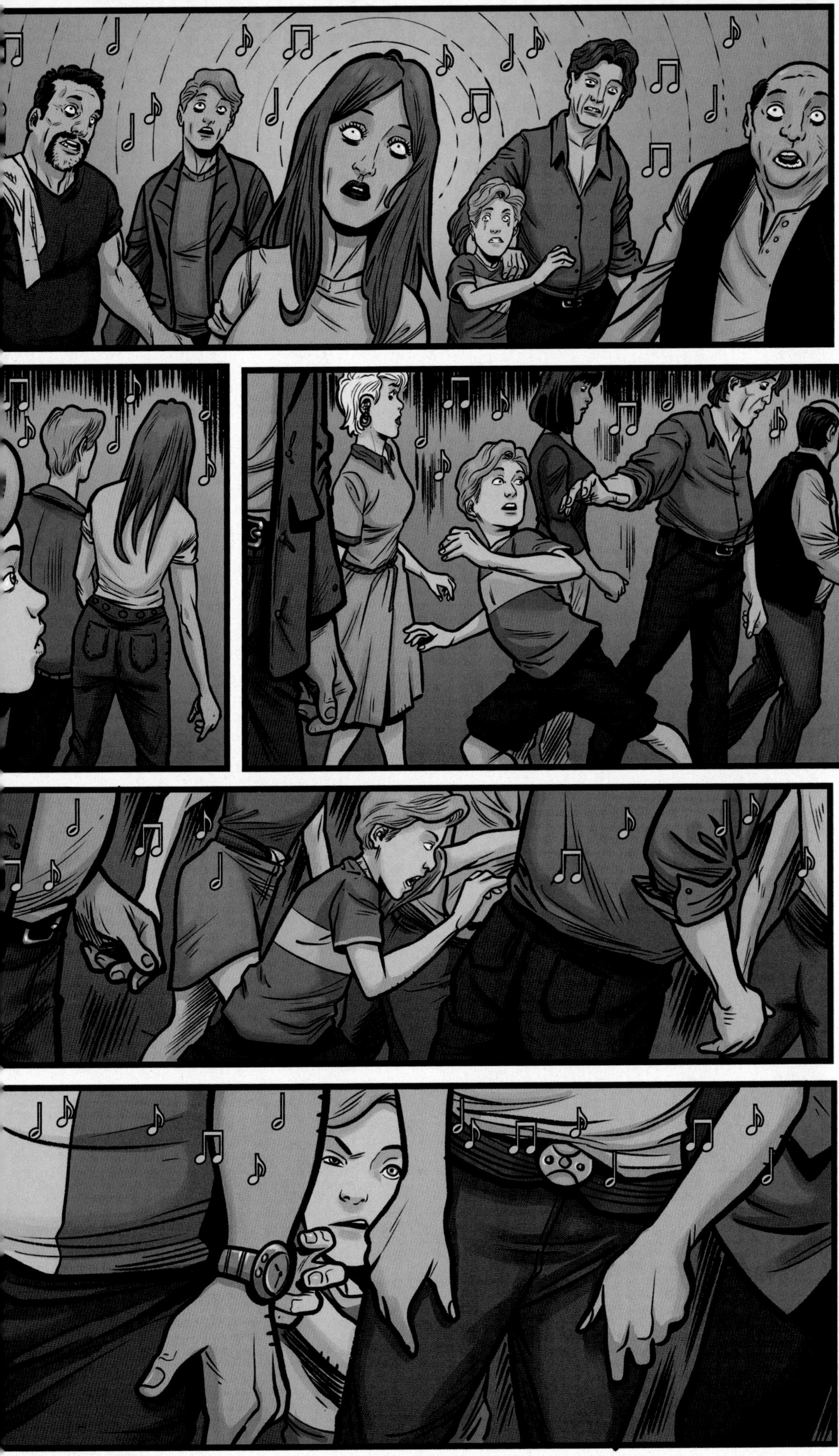

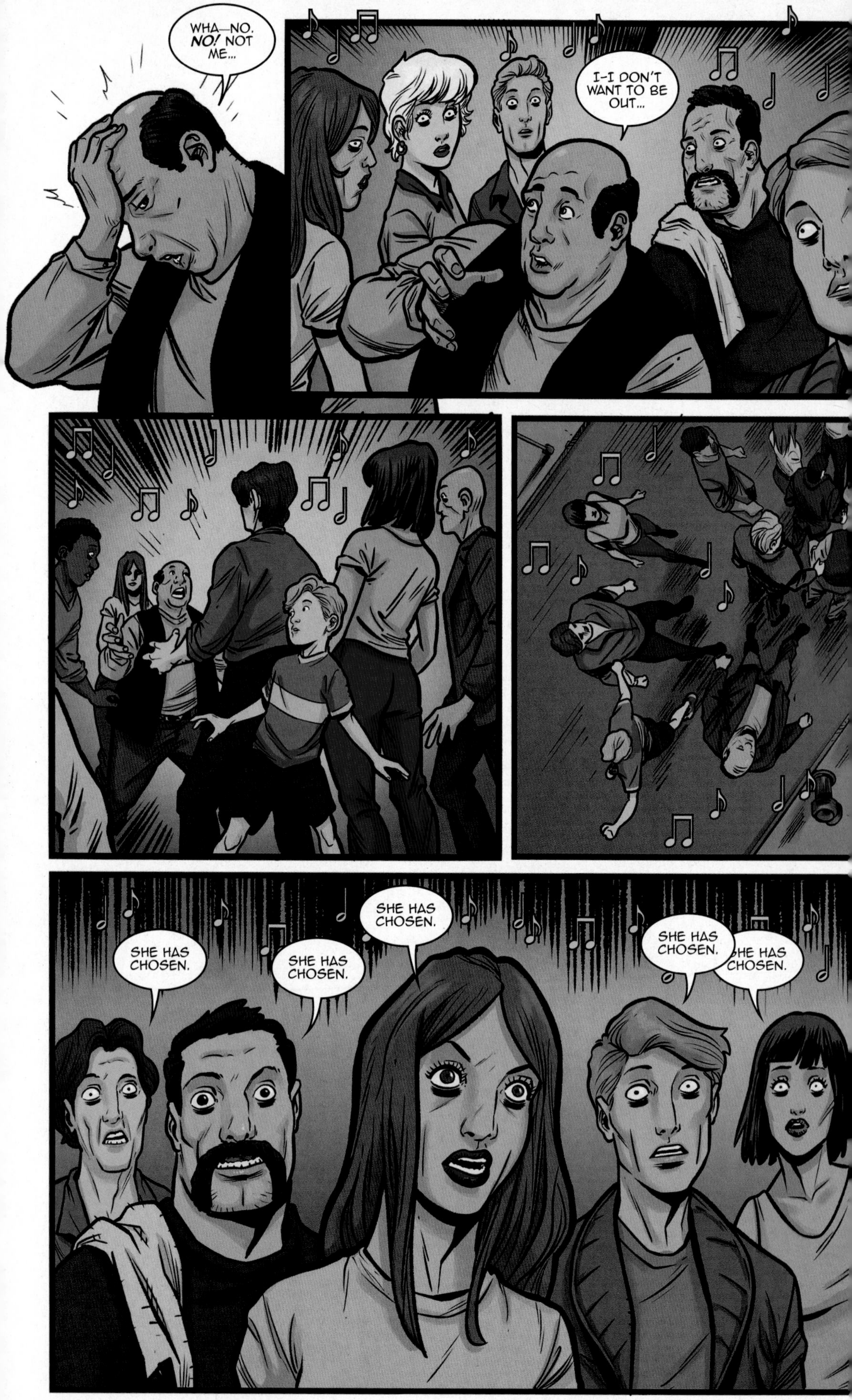
WHA—NO. **NO!** NOT ME...
I-I DON'T WANT TO BE OUT...
SHE HAS CHOSEN.
SHE HAS CHOSEN.
SHE HAS CHOSEN.
SHE HAS CHOSEN.
SHE HAS CHOSEN.

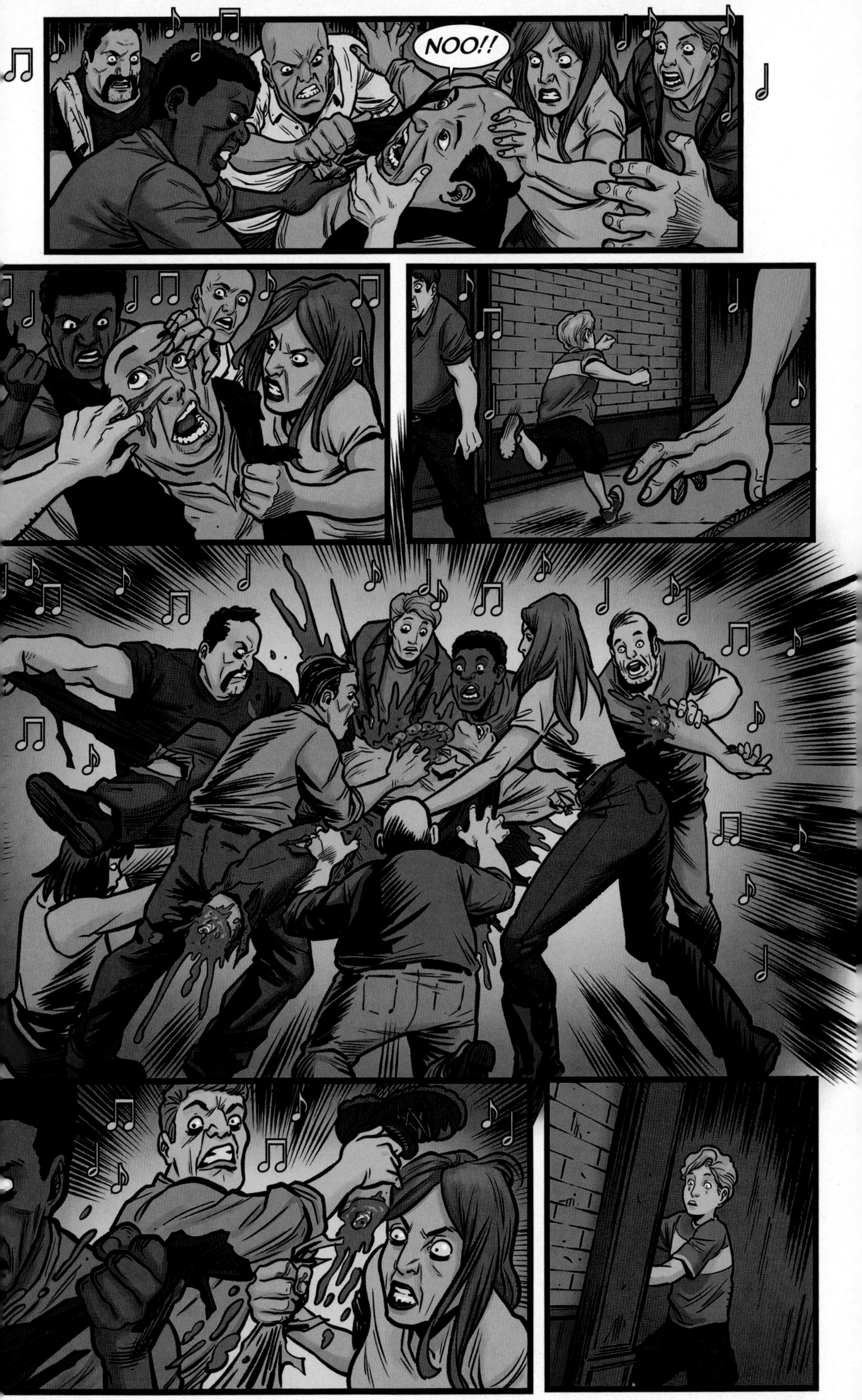
NOO!!

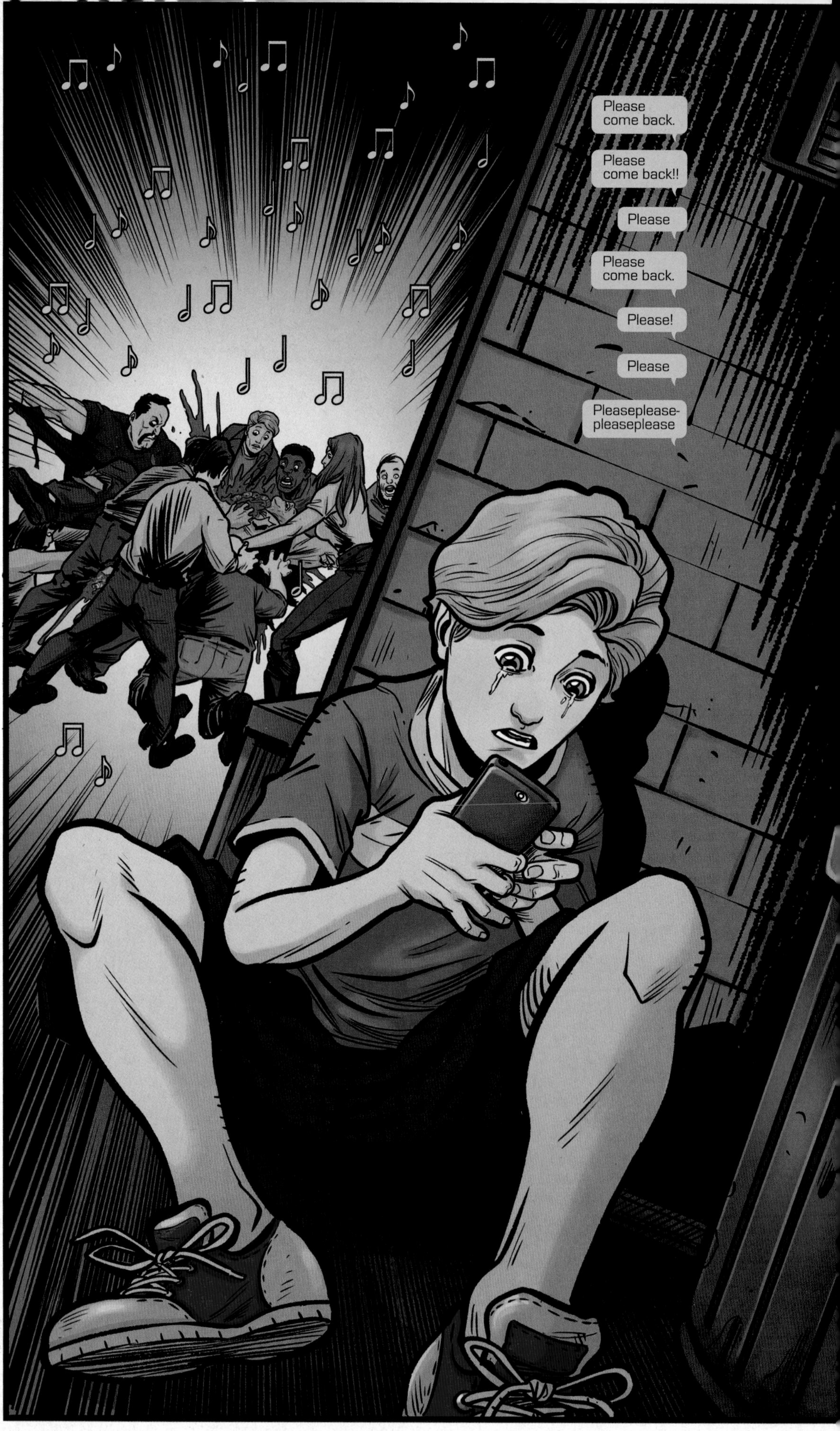
Please come back.
Please come back!!
Please
Please come back.
Please!
Please
Pleaseplease-pleaseplease

MUSICAL INTERLUDE

CHAPTER TWO

WRITTEN BY
SHAWN GABBORIN

ART BY
RAFAEL DANTAS

COLORS BY
ROSA "ROSAKAZ" RANTILA

SPECIAL THANKS TO DANIEL J. LOGAN

COVERS A & B
RAFAEL DANTAS
COVERS C & D
JOEL ADAMS
COVERS E & F
TONY FLEECS

Jason Martin: Publisher
Shawn Gabborin: Editor in Chief
Nicole D'Andria: Marketing Director/Editor
Danielle Davison: Executive Administrator
Bryan Seaton: CEO
Shawn Pryor: President of Creator Relations

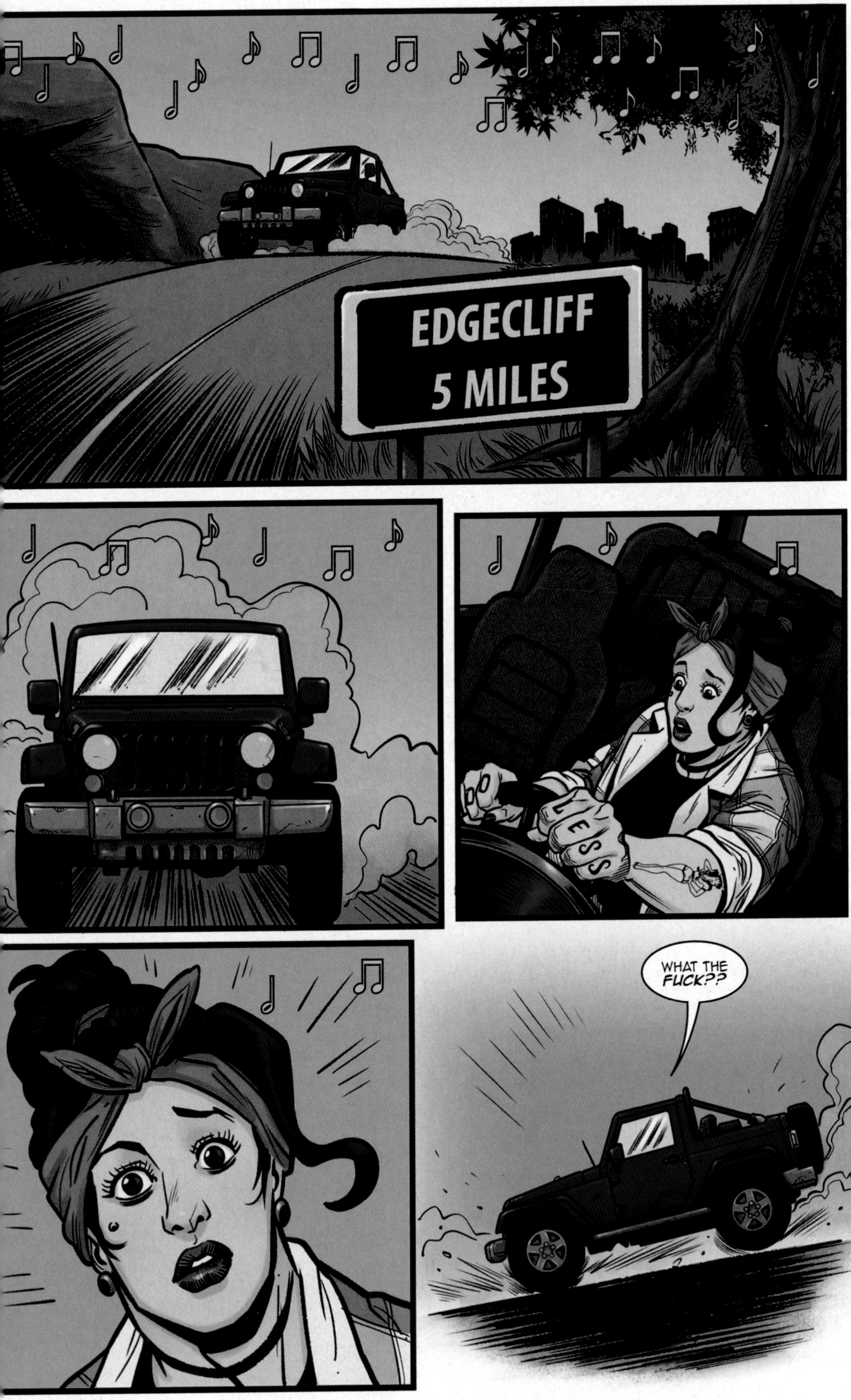
EDGECLIFF
5 MILES
LESS
WHAT THE FUCK??

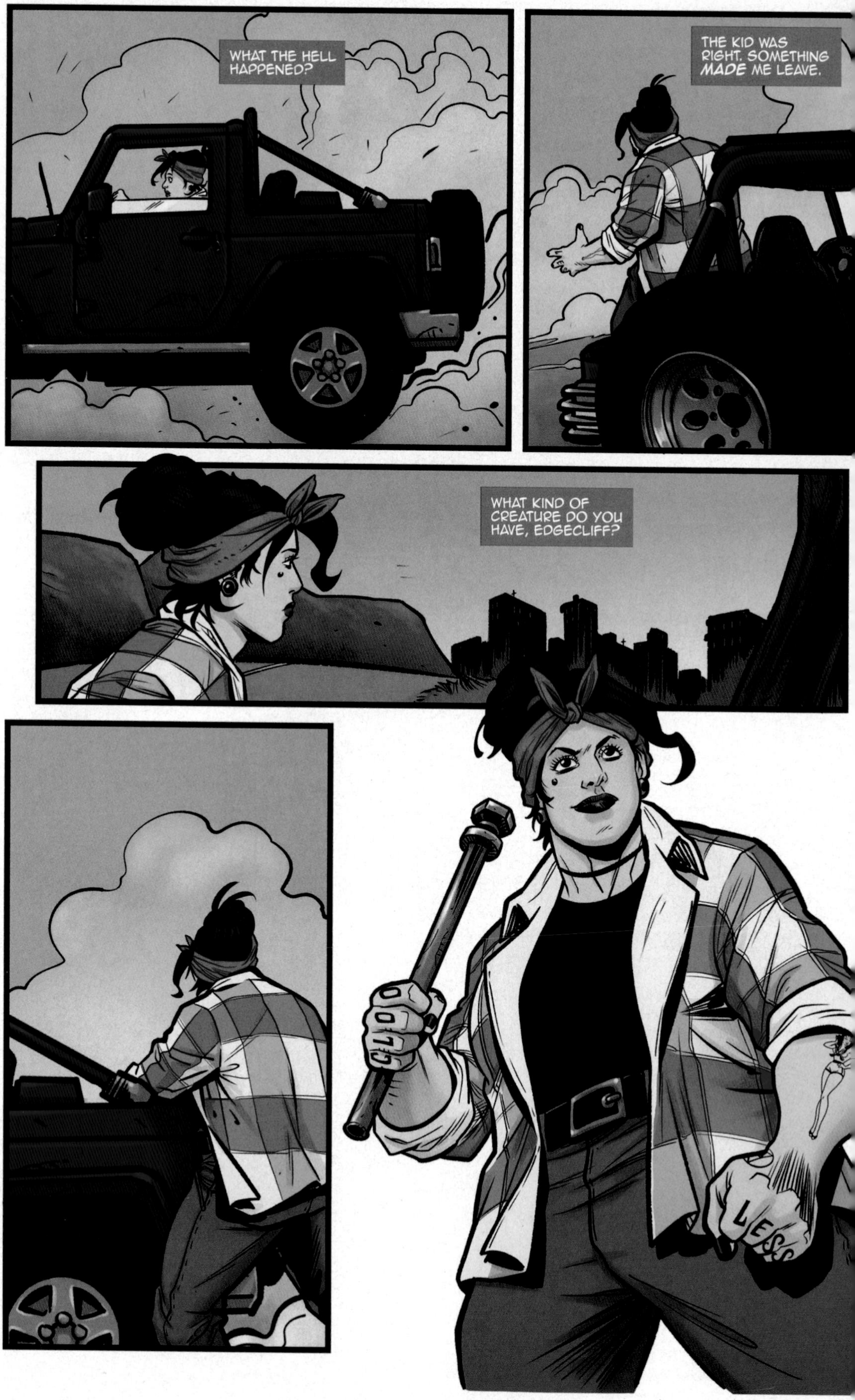
WHAT THE HELL HAPPENED?
THE KID WAS RIGHT. SOMETHING *MADE* ME LEAVE.
WHAT KIND OF CREATURE DO YOU HAVE, EDGECLIFF?
LESS

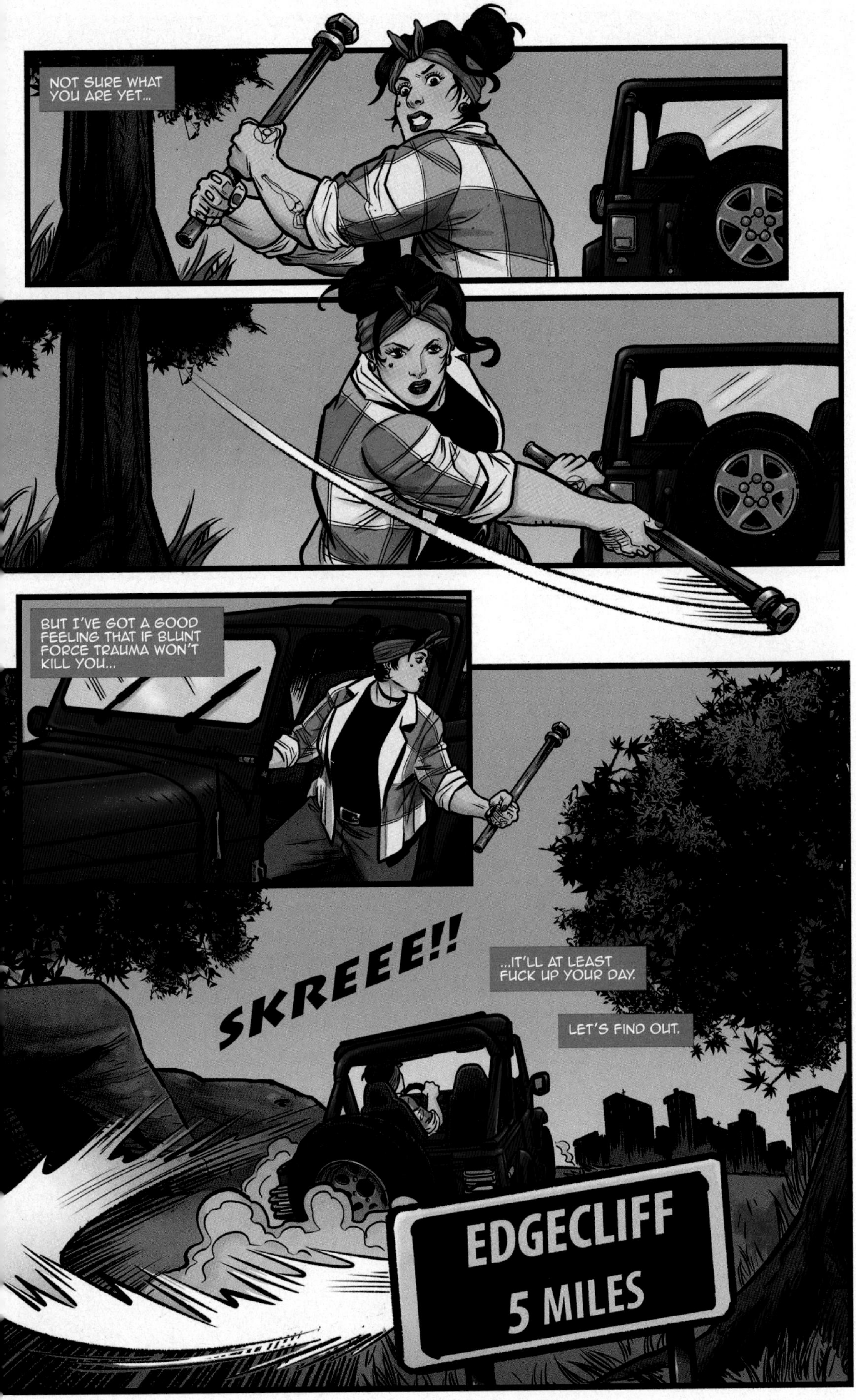
NOT SURE WHAT YOU ARE YET...
BUT I'VE GOT A GOOD FEELING THAT IF BLUNT FORCE TRAUMA WON'T KILL YOU...
SKREEE!!
...IT'LL AT LEAST FUCK UP YOUR DAY.
LET'S FIND OUT.
EDGECLIFF
5 MILES

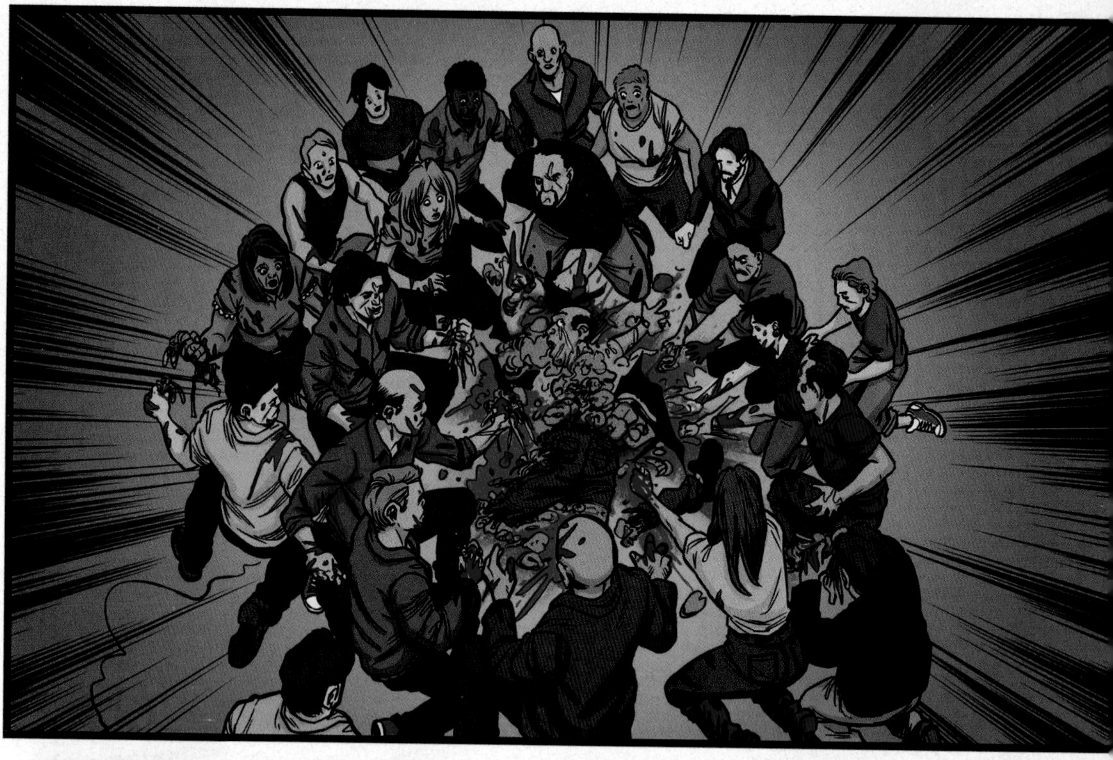

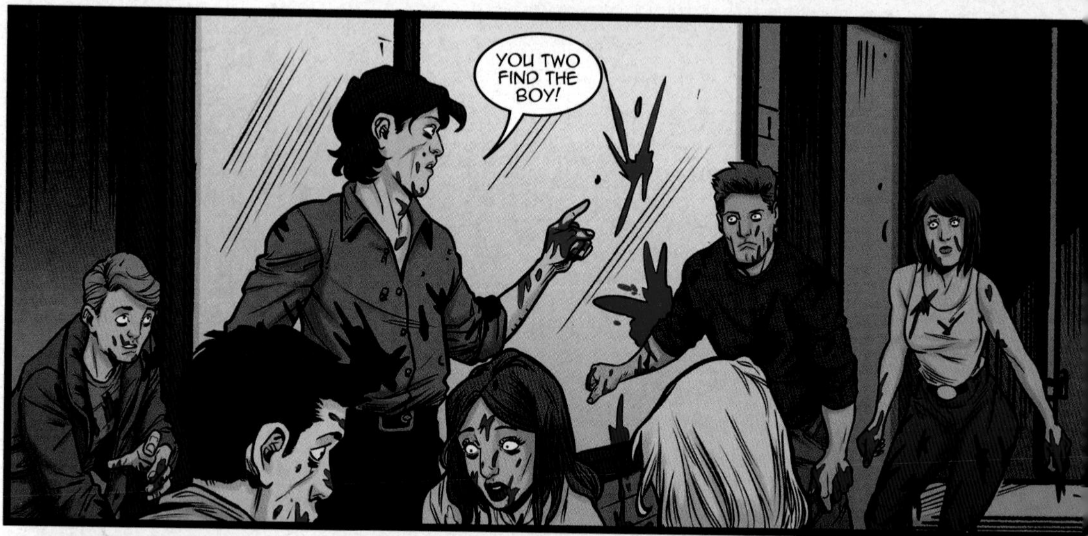
YOU TWO FIND THE BOY!

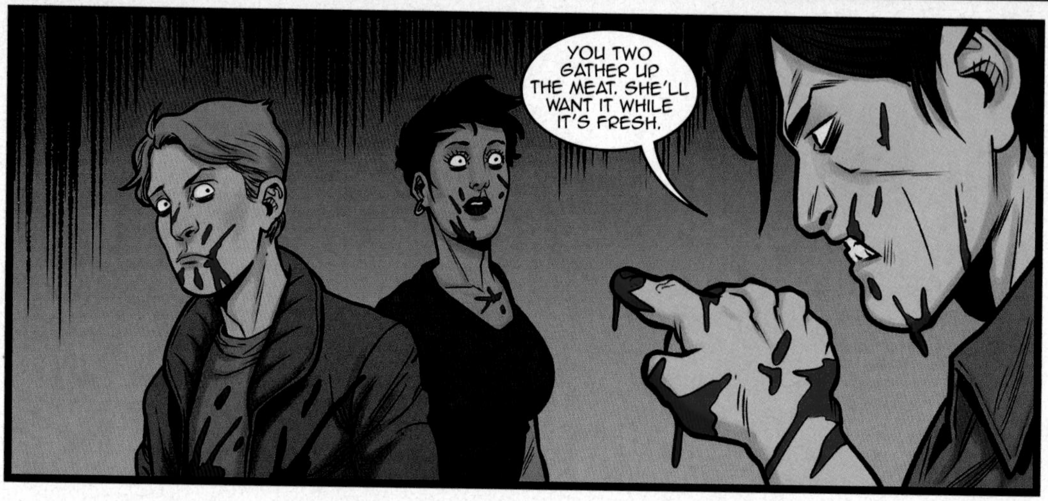
YOU TWO GATHER UP THE MEAT. SHE'LL WANT IT WHILE IT'S FRESH.

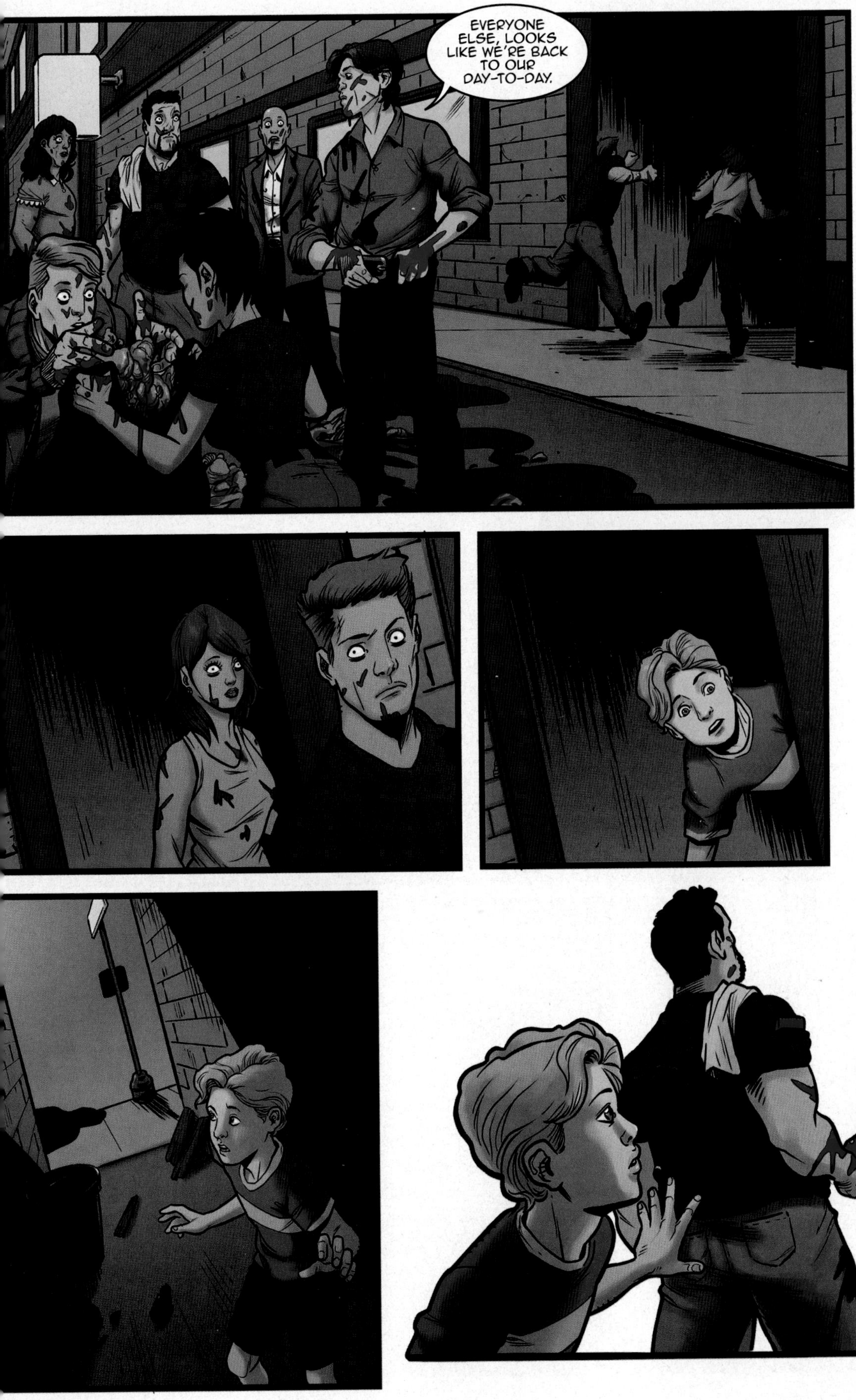
EVERYONE ELSE, LOOKS LIKE WE'RE BACK TO OUR DAY-TO-DAY.

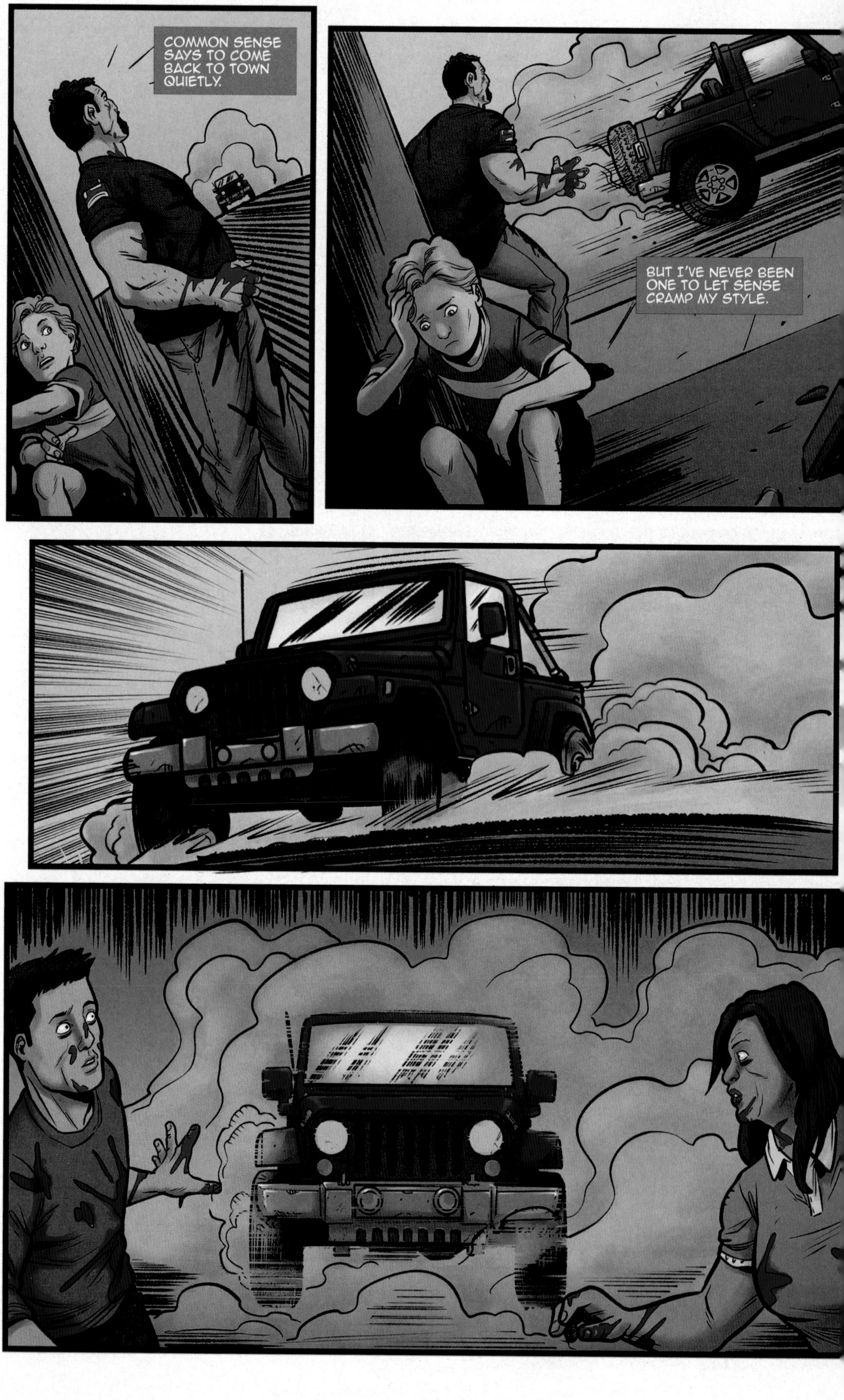
COMMON SENSE SAYS TO COME BACK TO TOWN QUIETLY.
BUT I'VE NEVER BEEN ONE TO LET SENSE CRAMP MY STYLE.

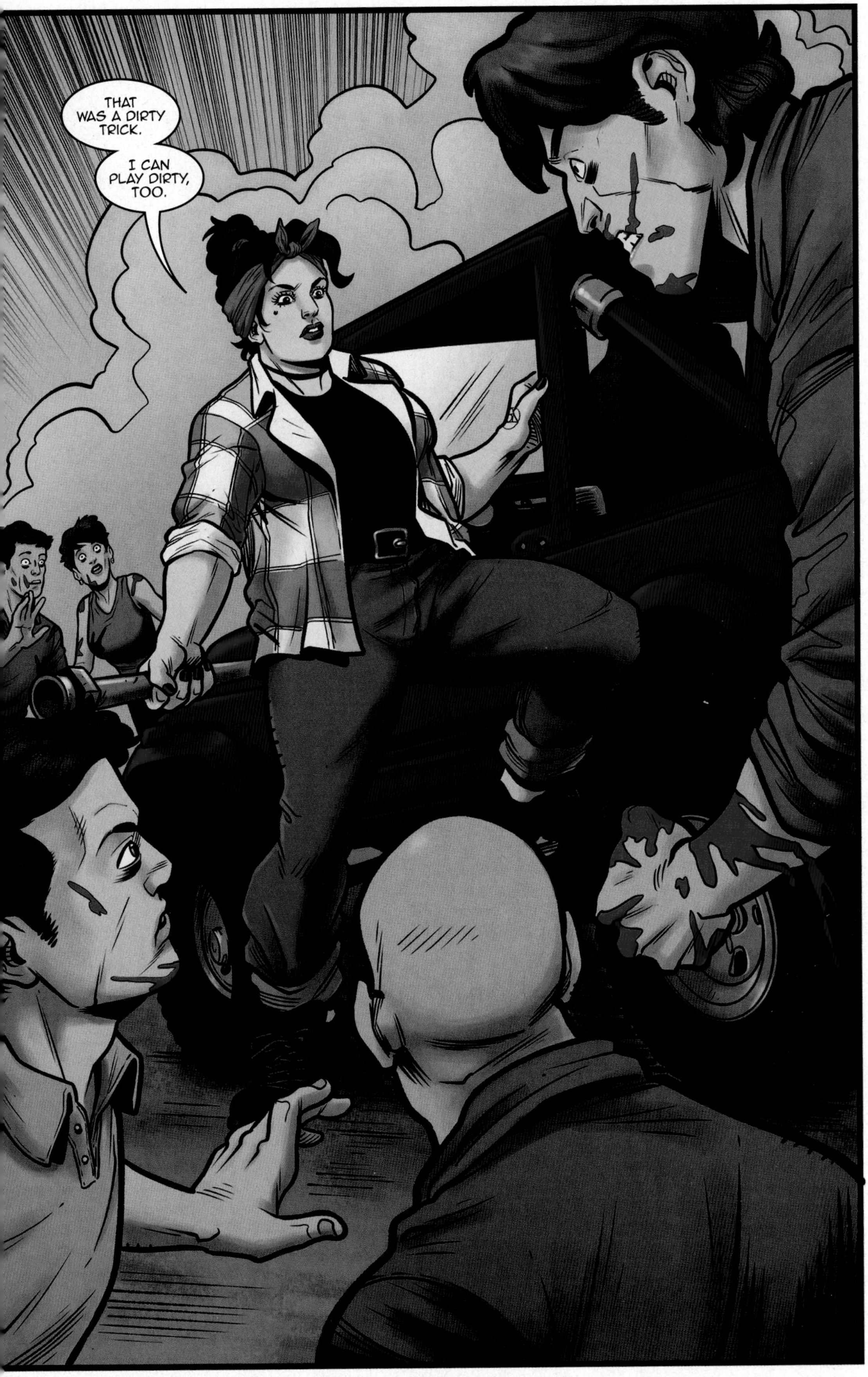
THAT WAS A DIRTY TRICK.
I CAN PLAY DIRTY, TOO.

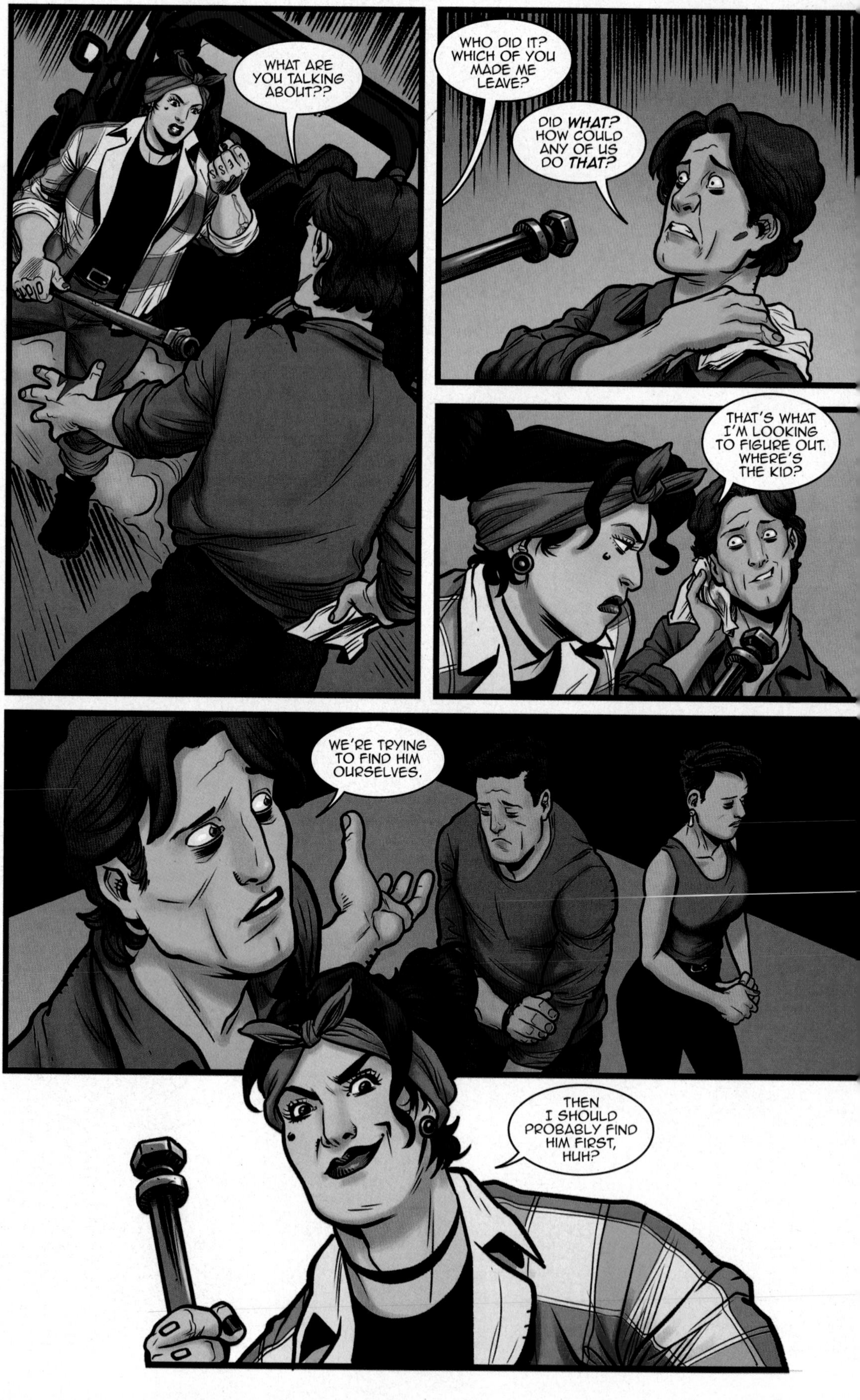
WHAT ARE YOU TALKING ABOUT??
WHO DID IT? WHICH OF YOU MADE ME LEAVE?
DID *WHAT?* HOW COULD ANY OF US DO *THAT?*
THAT'S WHAT I'M LOOKING TO FIGURE OUT. WHERE'S THE KID?
WE'RE TRYING TO FIND HIM OURSELVES.
THEN I SHOULD PROBABLY FIND HIM FIRST, HUH?

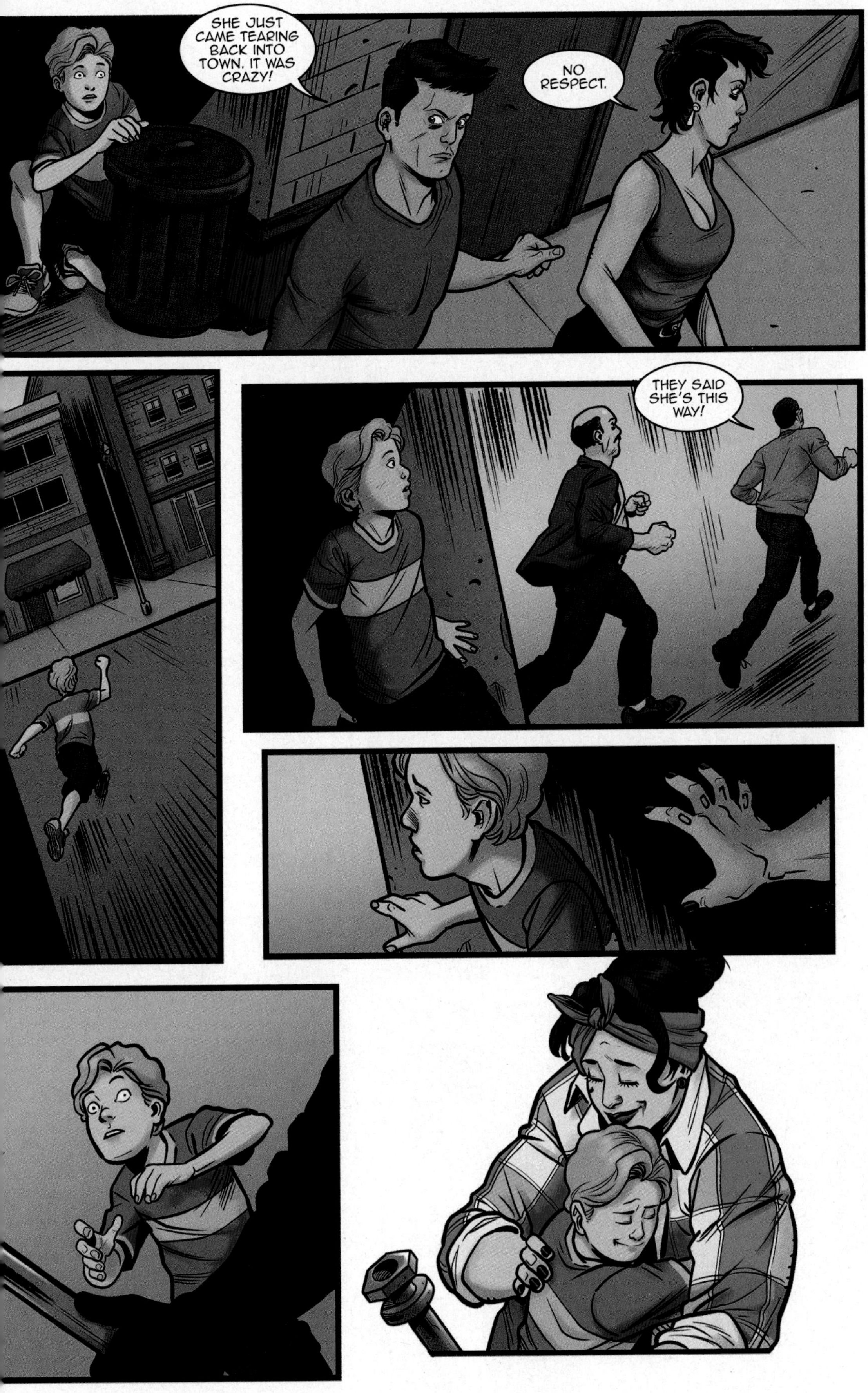
SHE JUST CAME TEARING BACK INTO TOWN. IT WAS CRAZY!
NO RESPECT.
THEY SAID SHE'S THIS WAY!

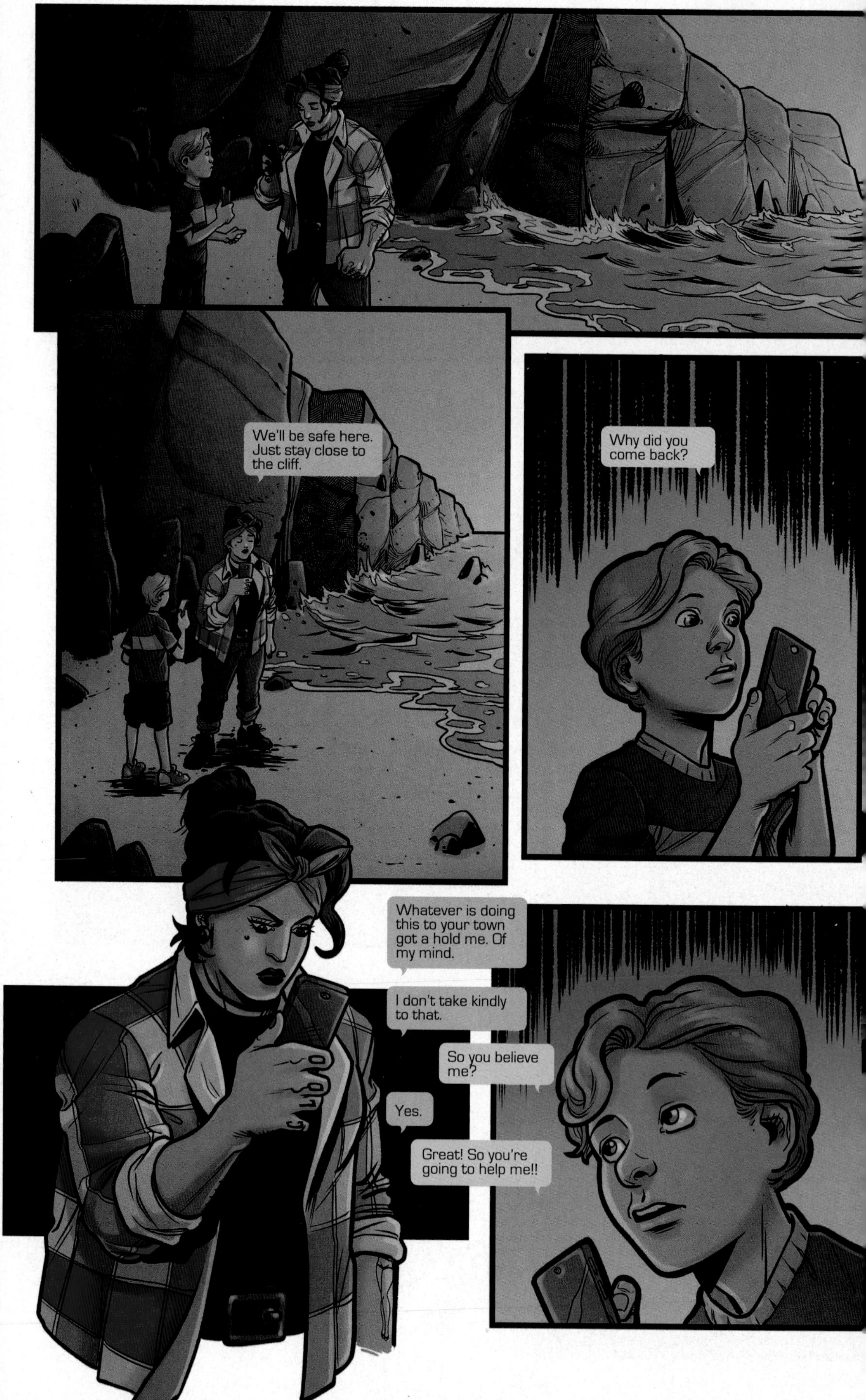
We'll be safe here. Just stay close to the cliff.
Why did you come back?
Whatever is doing this to your town got a hold me. Of my mind.
I don't take kindly to that.
So you believe me?
Yes.
Great! So you're going to help me!!

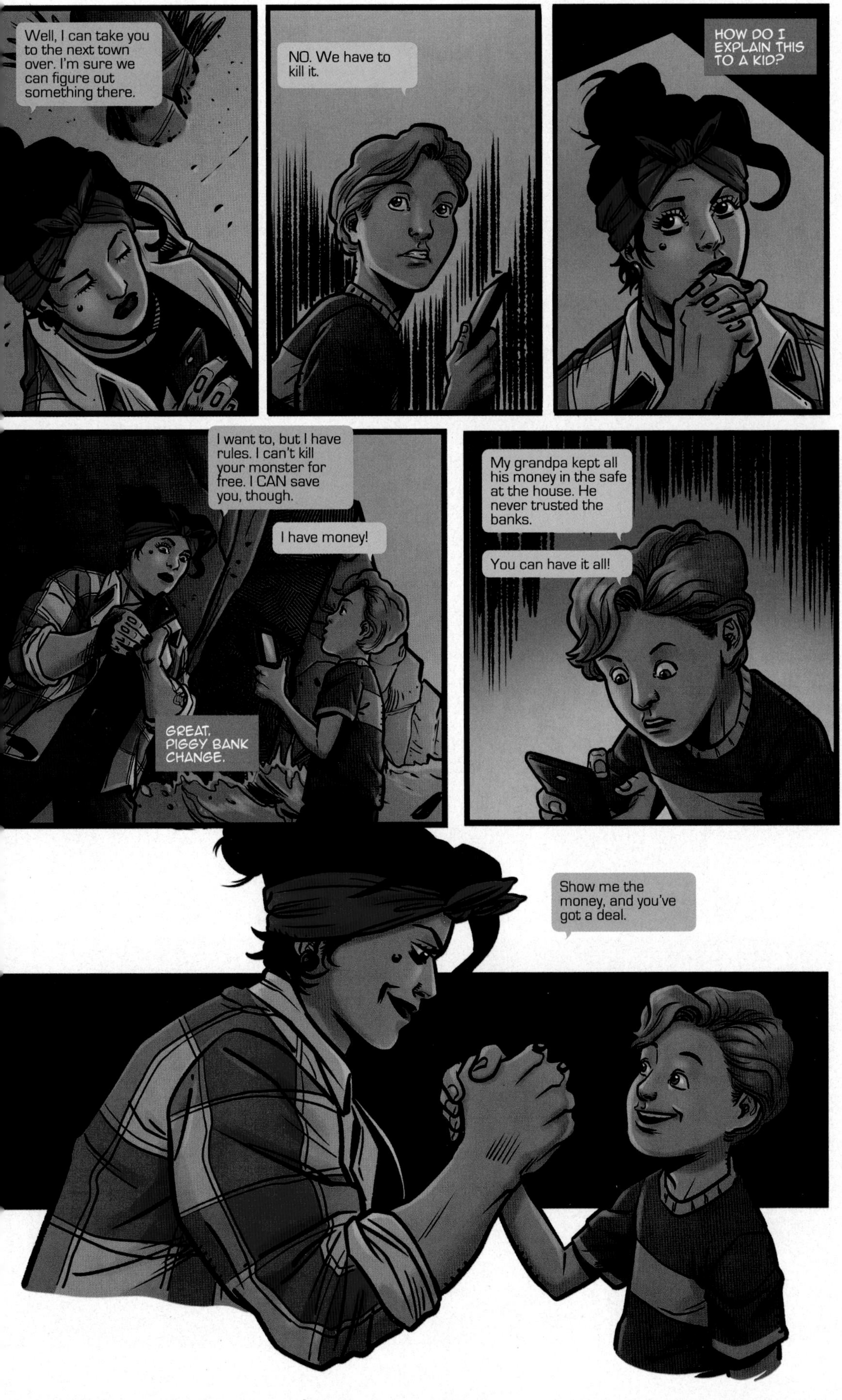
Well, I can take you to the next town over. I'm sure we can figure out something there.
NO. We have to kill it.
HOW DO I EXPLAIN THIS TO A KID?
I want to, but I have rules. I can't kill your monster for free. I CAN save you, though.
I have money!
GREAT. PIGGY BANK CHANGE.
My grandpa kept all his money in the safe at the house. He never trusted the banks.
You can have it all!
Show me the money, and you've got a deal.

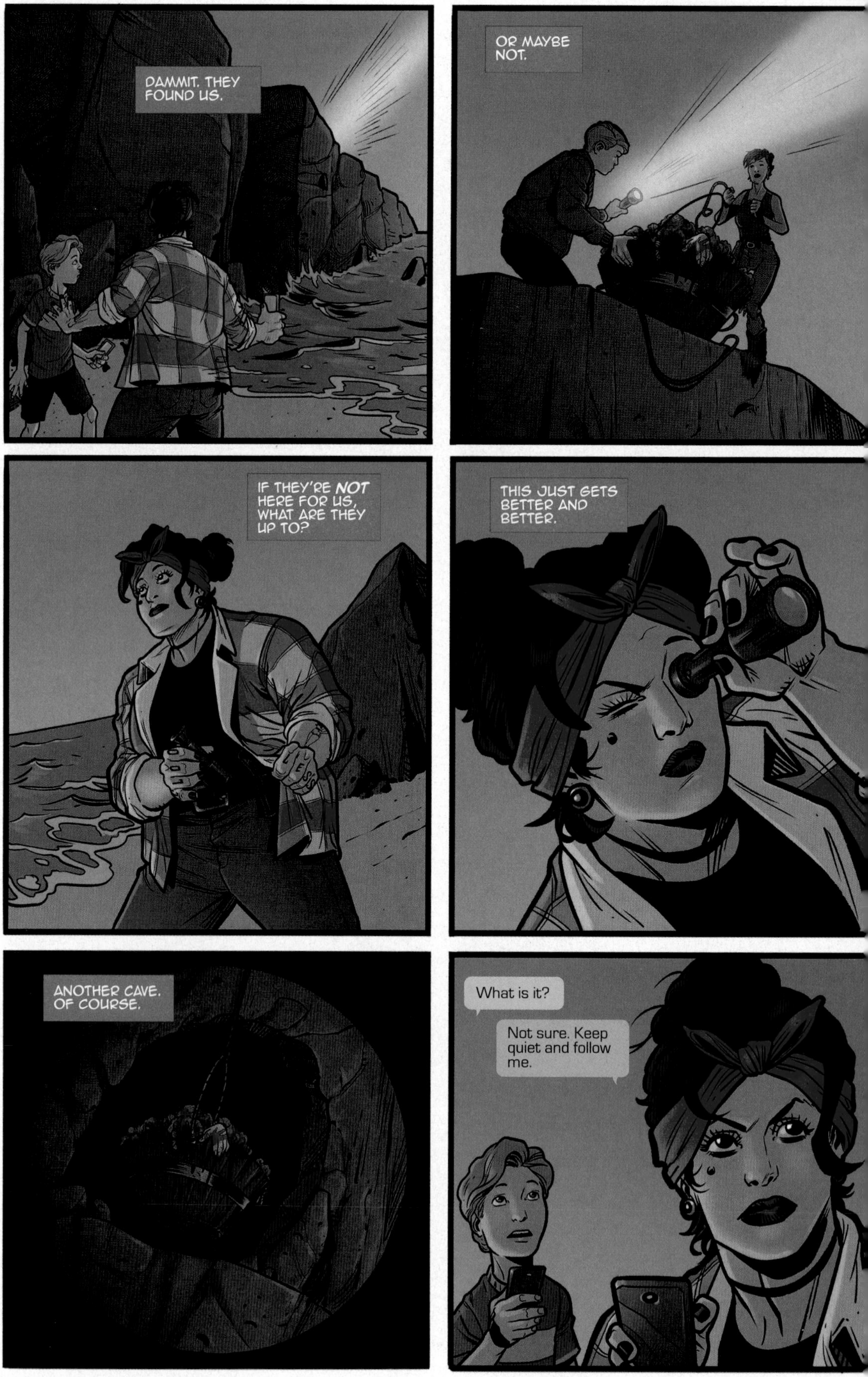
DAMMIT. THEY FOUND US.
OR MAYBE NOT.
IF THEY'RE *NOT* HERE FOR US, WHAT ARE THEY UP TO?
THIS JUST GETS BETTER AND BETTER.
ANOTHER CAVE. OF COURSE.
What is it?
Not sure. Keep quiet and follow me.

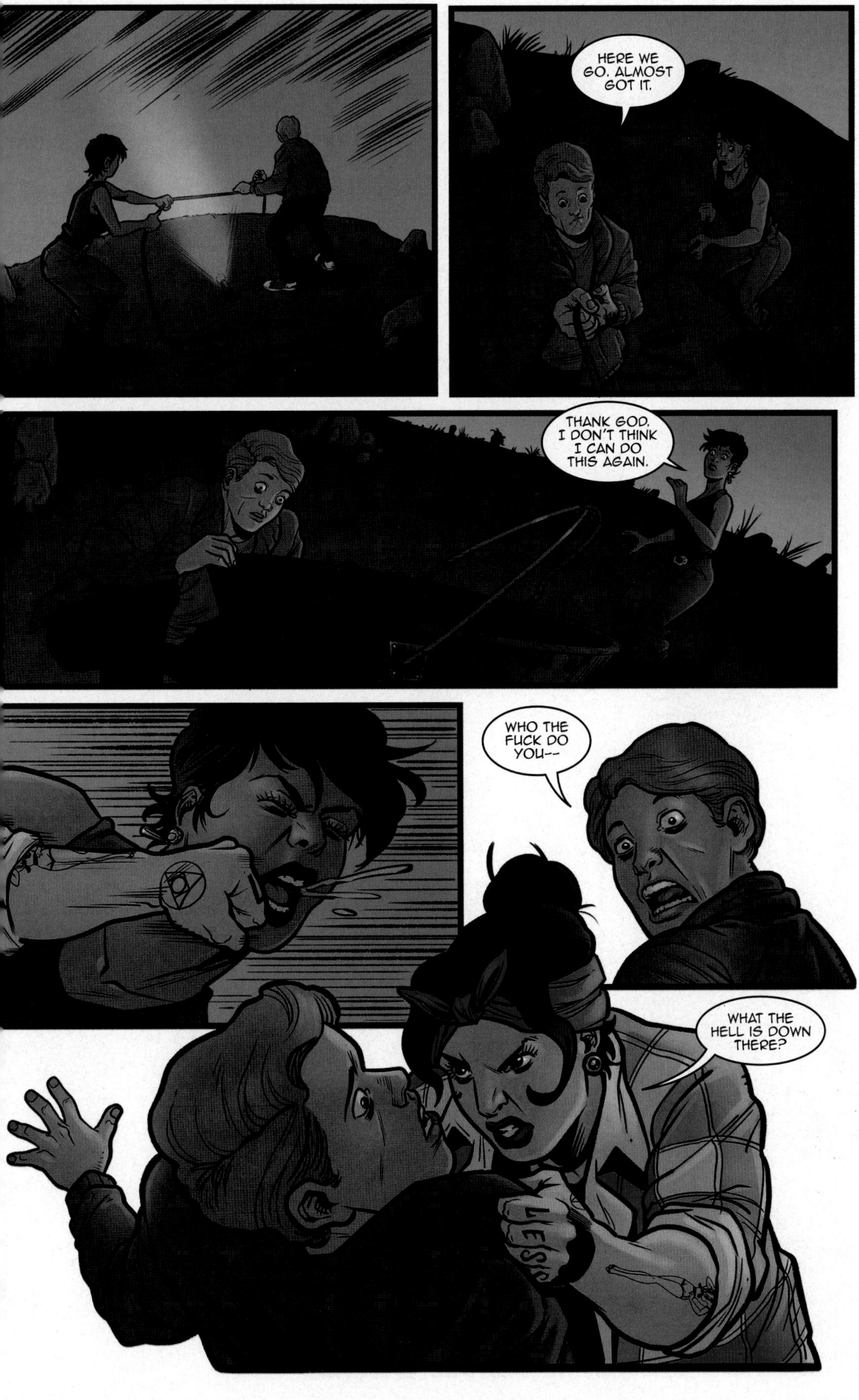
HERE WE GO. ALMOST GOT IT.
THANK GOD. I DON'T THINK I CAN DO THIS AGAIN.
WHO THE FUCK DO YOU--
WHAT THE HELL IS DOWN THERE?
LIES

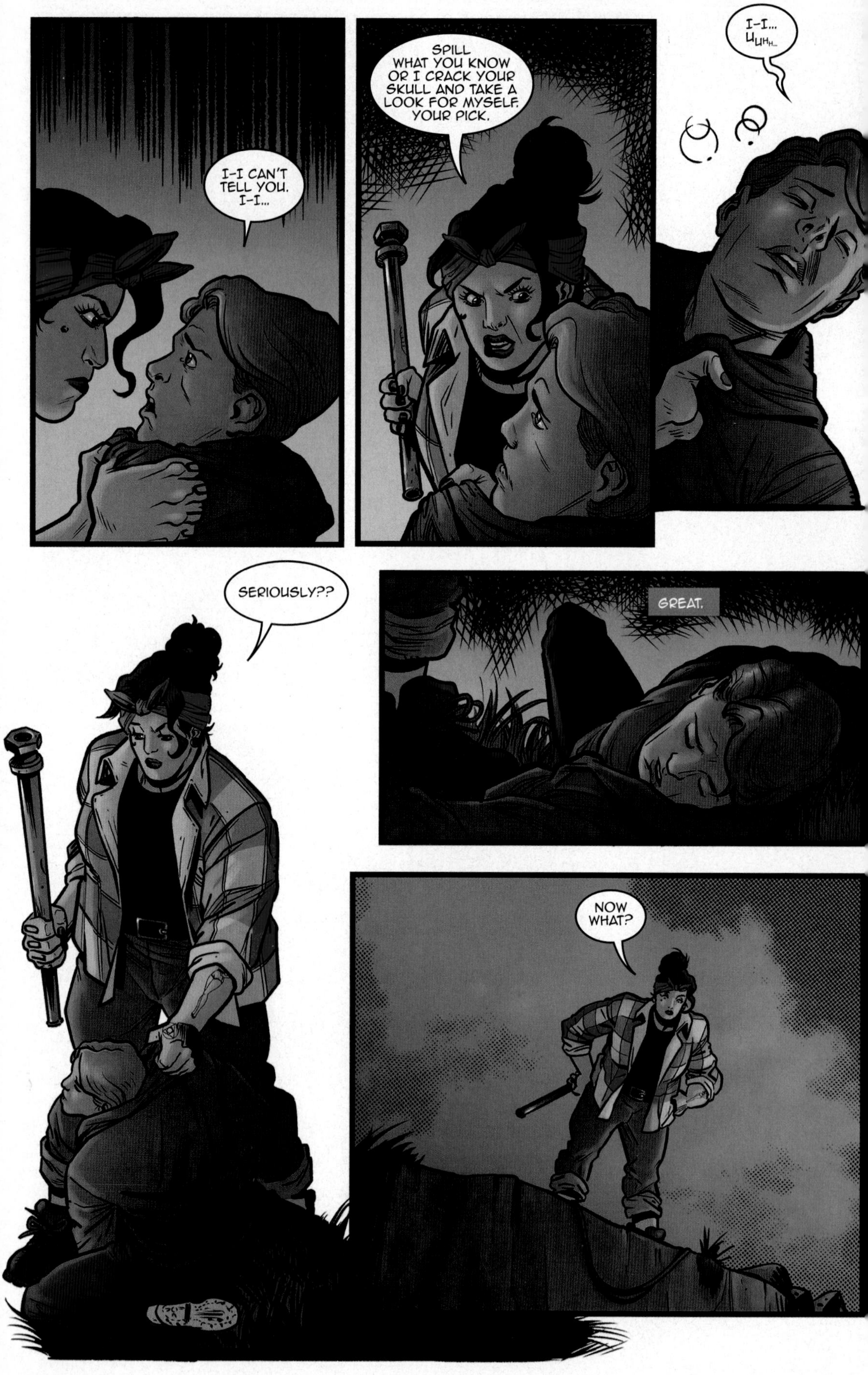
I-I CAN'T TELL YOU. I-I...
SPILL WHAT YOU KNOW OR I CRACK YOUR SKULL AND TAKE A LOOK FOR MYSELF. YOUR PICK.
I-I... UHHH...
SERIOUSLY??
GREAT.
NOW WHAT?

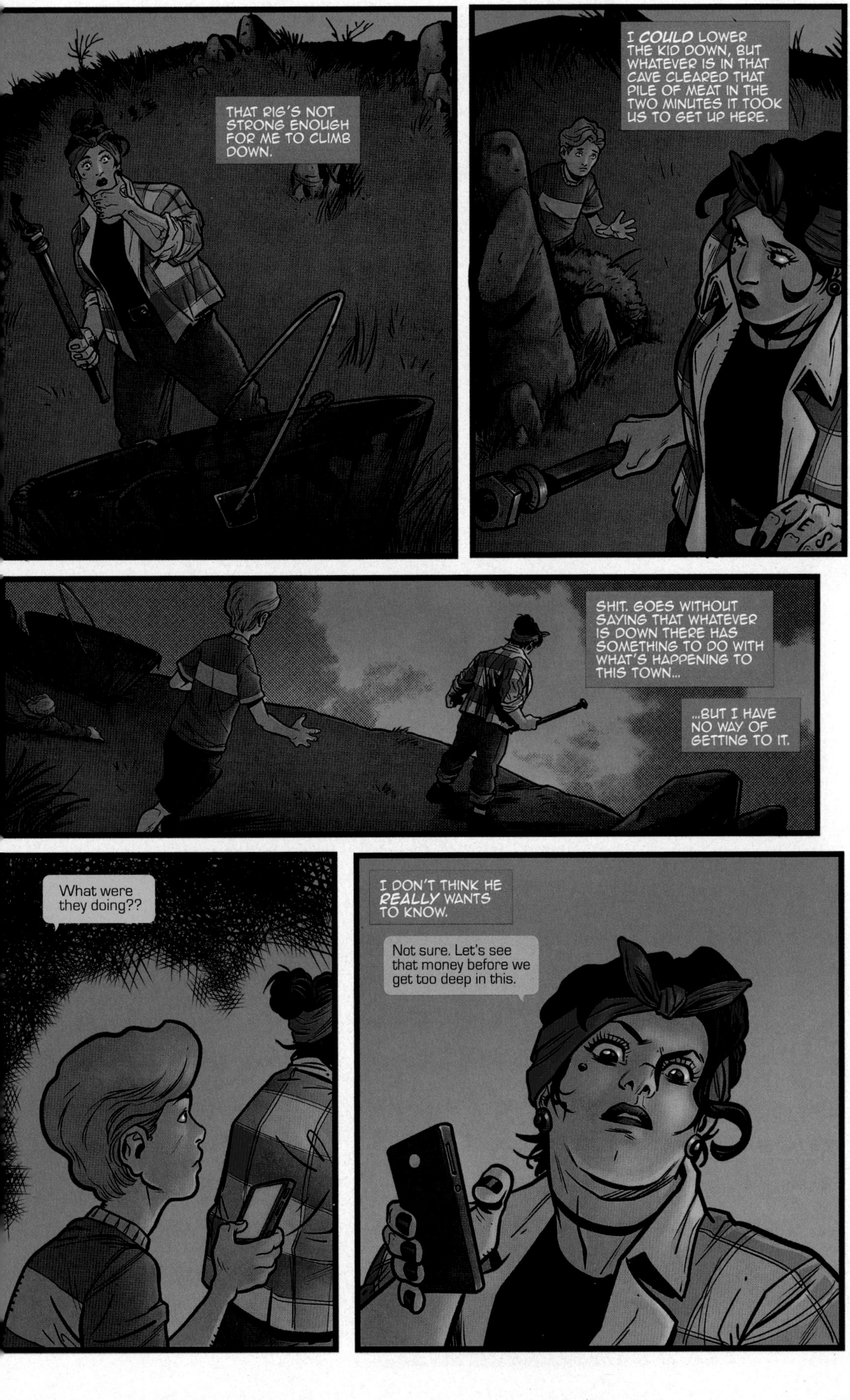

THAT RIG'S NOT STRONG ENOUGH FOR ME TO CLIMB DOWN.
I COULD LOWER THE KID DOWN, BUT WHATEVER IS IN THAT CAVE CLEARED THAT PILE OF MEAT IN THE TWO MINUTES IT TOOK US TO GET UP HERE.
SHIT. GOES WITHOUT SAYING THAT WHATEVER IS DOWN THERE HAS SOMETHING TO DO WITH WHAT'S HAPPENING TO THIS TOWN...
...BUT I HAVE NO WAY OF GETTING TO IT.
What were they doing??
I DON'T THINK HE REALLY WANTS TO KNOW.
Not sure. Let's see that money before we get too deep in this.

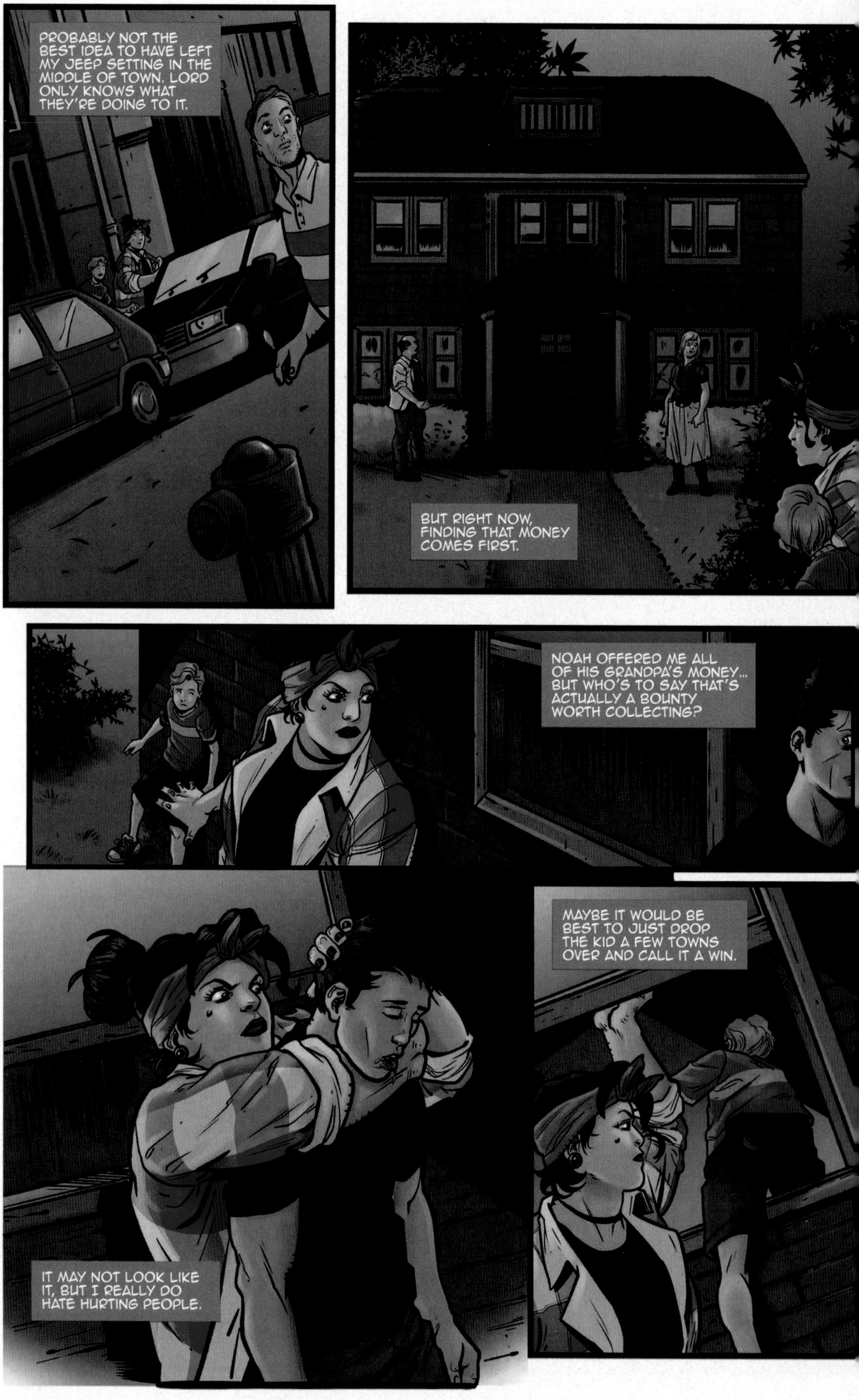
PROBABLY NOT THE BEST IDEA TO HAVE LEFT MY JEEP SETTING IN THE MIDDLE OF TOWN. LORD ONLY KNOWS WHAT THEY'RE DOING TO IT.
BUT RIGHT NOW, FINDING THAT MONEY COMES FIRST.
NOAH OFFERED ME ALL OF HIS GRANDPA'S MONEY... BUT WHO'S TO SAY THAT'S ACTUALLY A BOUNTY WORTH COLLECTING?
IT MAY NOT LOOK LIKE IT, BUT I REALLY DO HATE HURTING PEOPLE.
MAYBE IT WOULD BE BEST TO JUST DROP THE KID A FEW TOWNS OVER AND CALL IT A WIN.

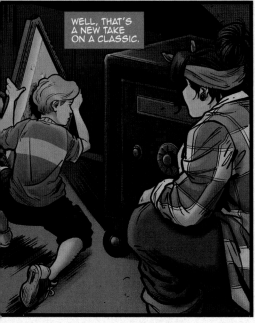

WELL, THAT'S A NEW TAKE ON A CLASSIC.

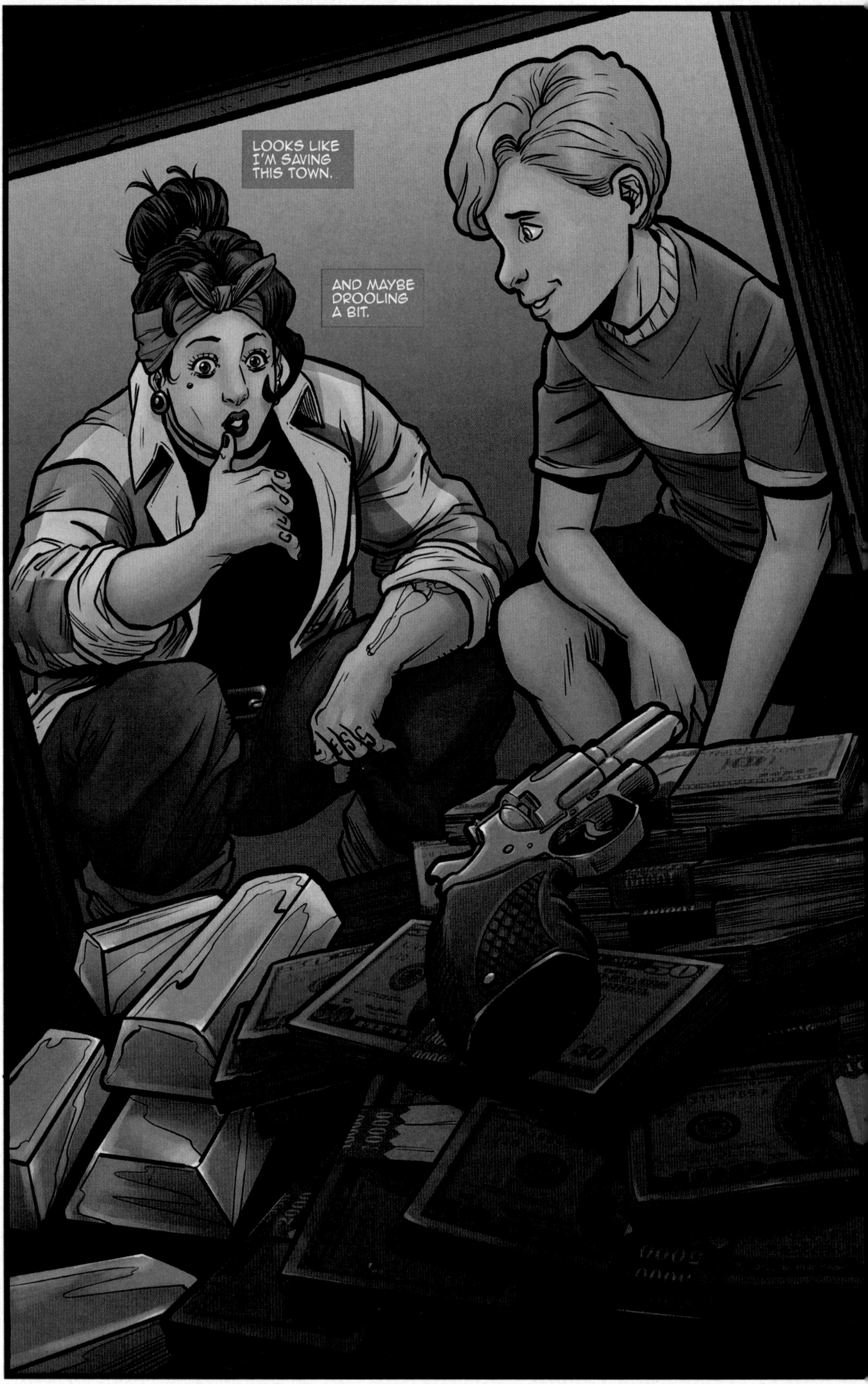
LOOKS LIKE I'M SAVING THIS TOWN.
AND MAYBE DROOLING A BIT.

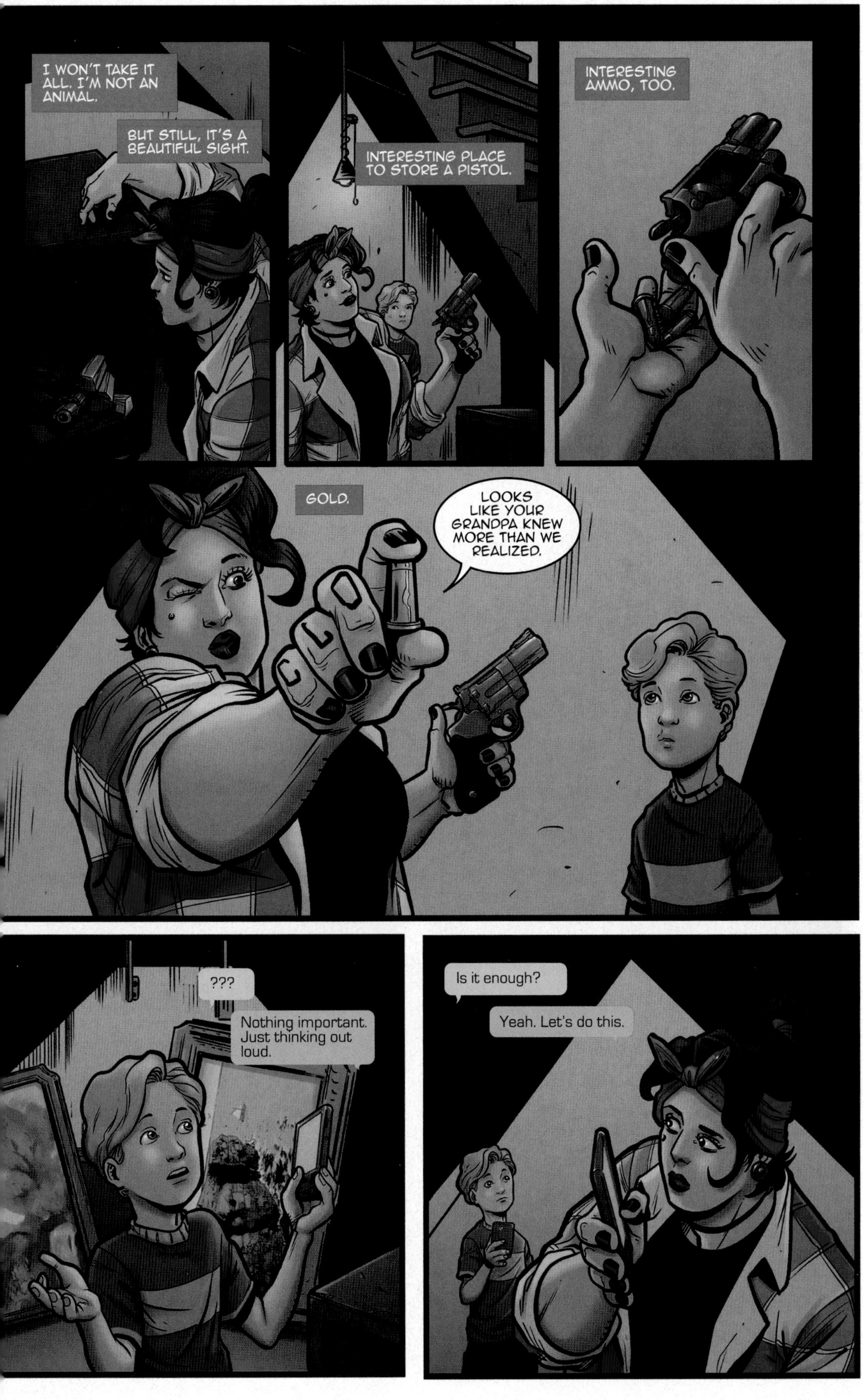
I WON'T TAKE IT ALL. I'M NOT AN ANIMAL.
BUT STILL, IT'S A BEAUTIFUL SIGHT.
INTERESTING PLACE TO STORE A PISTOL.
INTERESTING AMMO, TOO.
GOLD.
LOOKS LIKE YOUR GRANDPA KNEW MORE THAN WE REALIZED.
???
Nothing important. Just thinking out loud.
Is it enough?
Yeah. Let's do this.

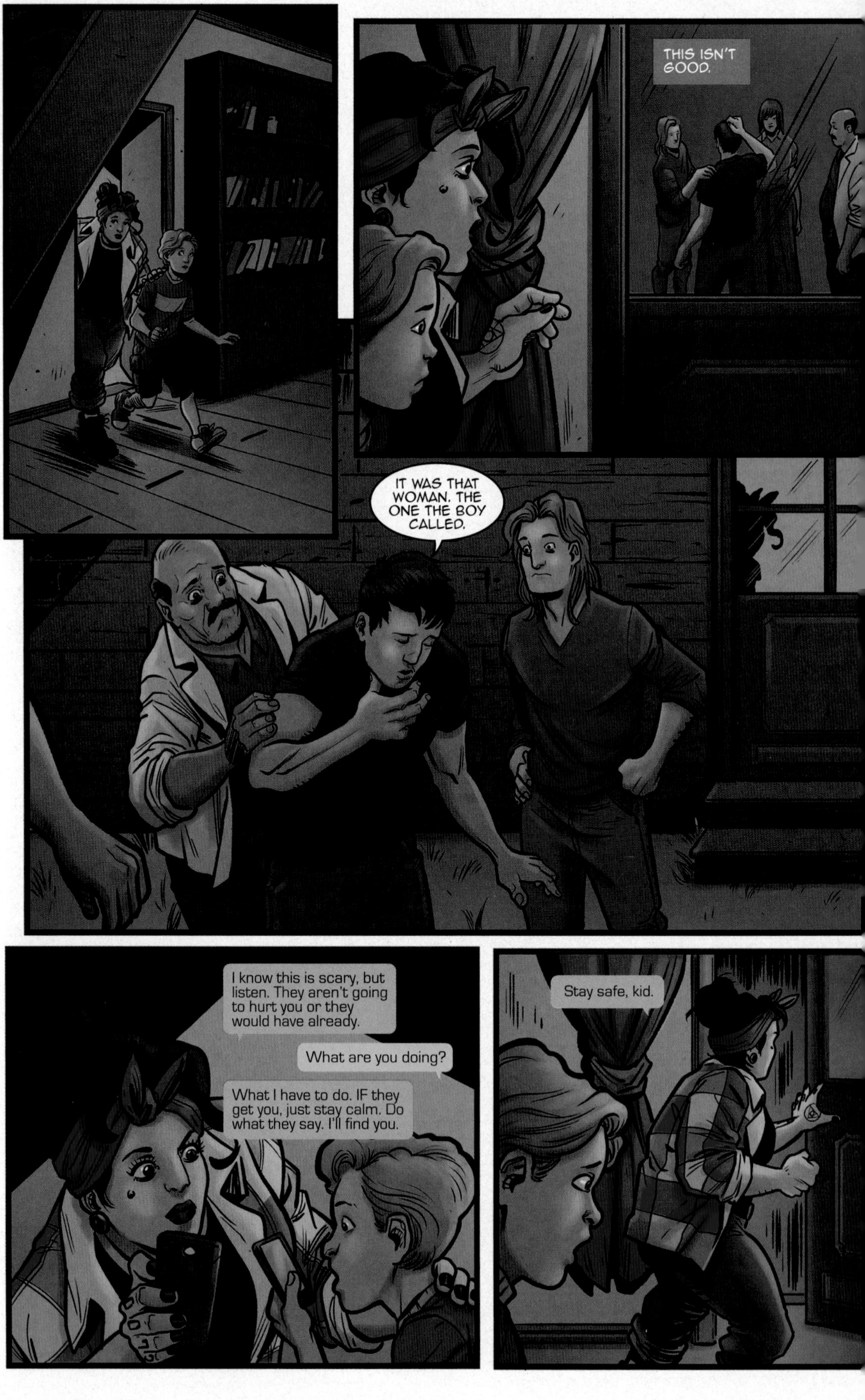
THIS ISN'T GOOD.
IT WAS THAT WOMAN. THE ONE THE BOY CALLED.
I know this is scary, but listen. They aren't going to hurt you or they would have already.
What are you doing?
What I have to do. IF they get you, just stay calm. Do what they say. I'll find you.
Stay safe, kid.

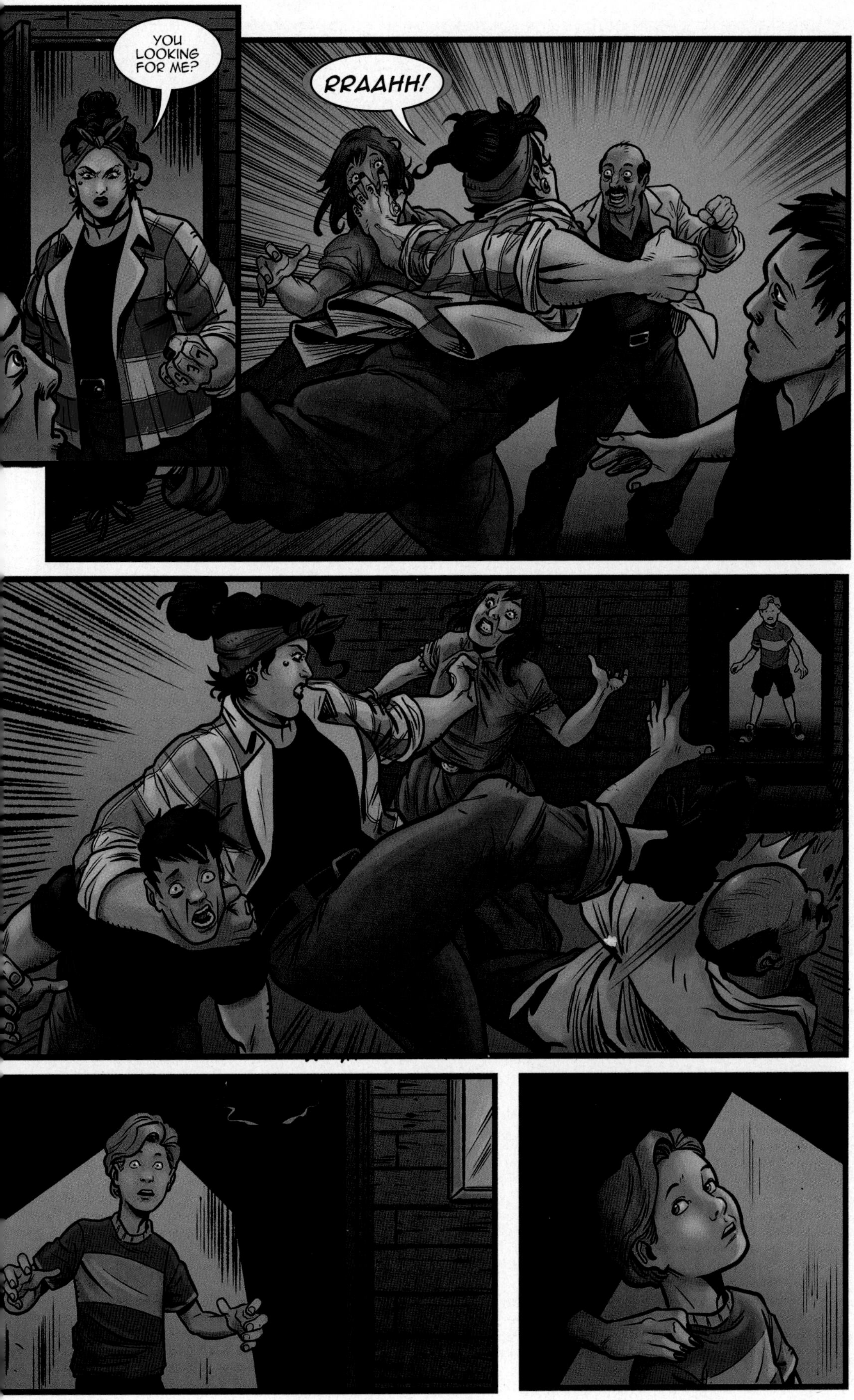
YOU LOOKING FOR ME?
RRAAHH!

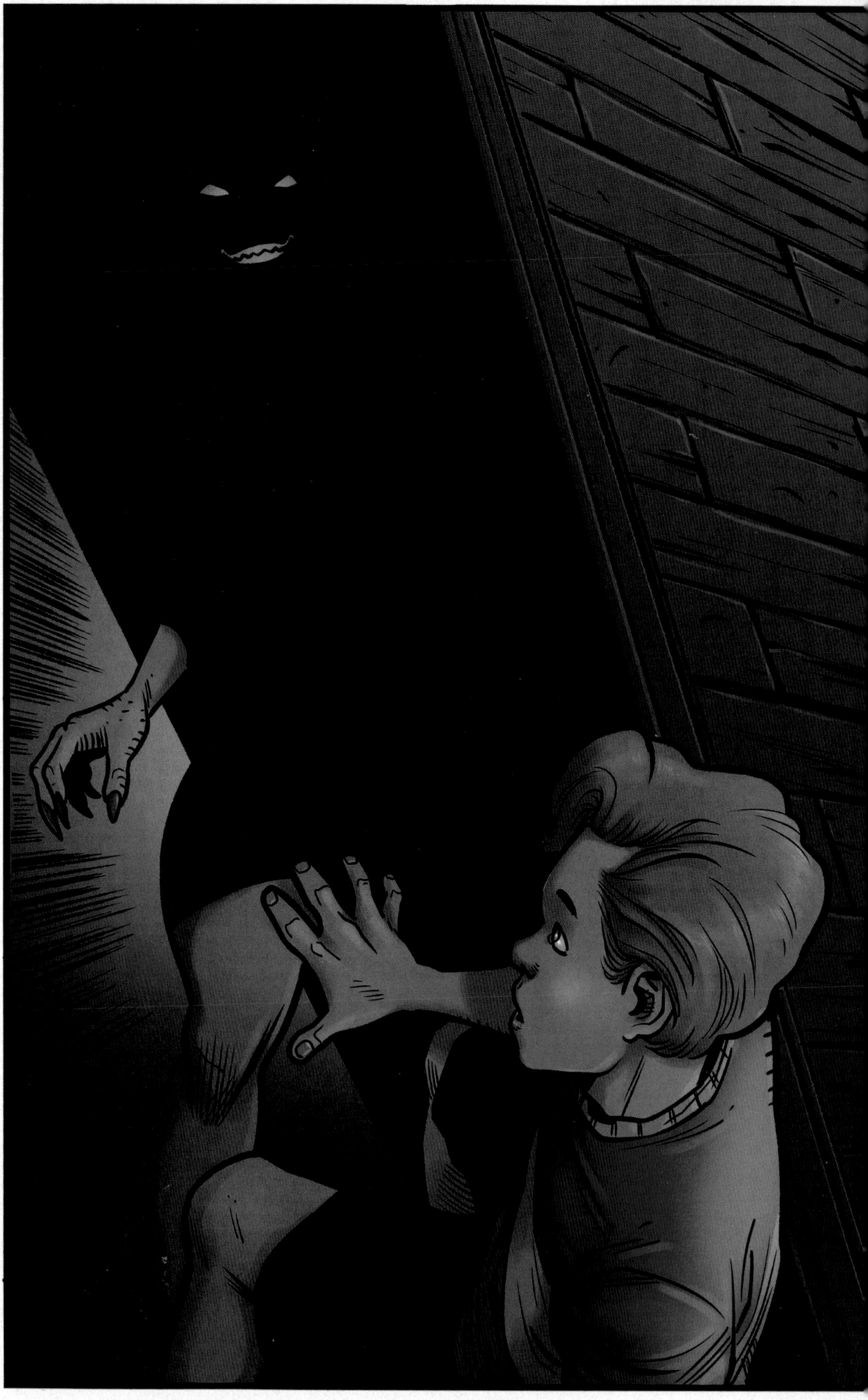

MUSICAL INTERLUDE

CHAPTER THREE

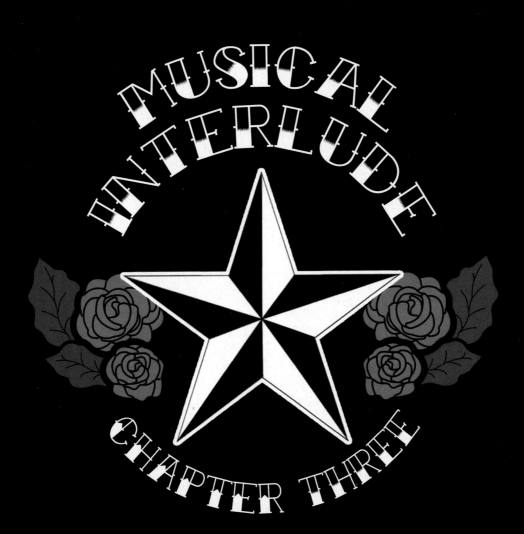

WRITTEN BY
SHAWN GABBORIN

ART BY
RAFAEL DANTAS

COLORS BY
ROSA "ROSAKAZ" RANTILA

SPECIAL THANKS TO DANIEL J. LOGAN

COVERS A & B
RAFAEL DANTAS

COVERS C & D
ANN ULAND

COVERS E & F
ZOE STANLEY

Jason Martin: Publisher
Shawn Gabborin: Editor in Chief
Nicole D'Andria: Marketing Director/Editor
Danielle Davison: Executive Administrator
Bryan Seaton: CEO
Shawn Pryor: President of Creator Relations

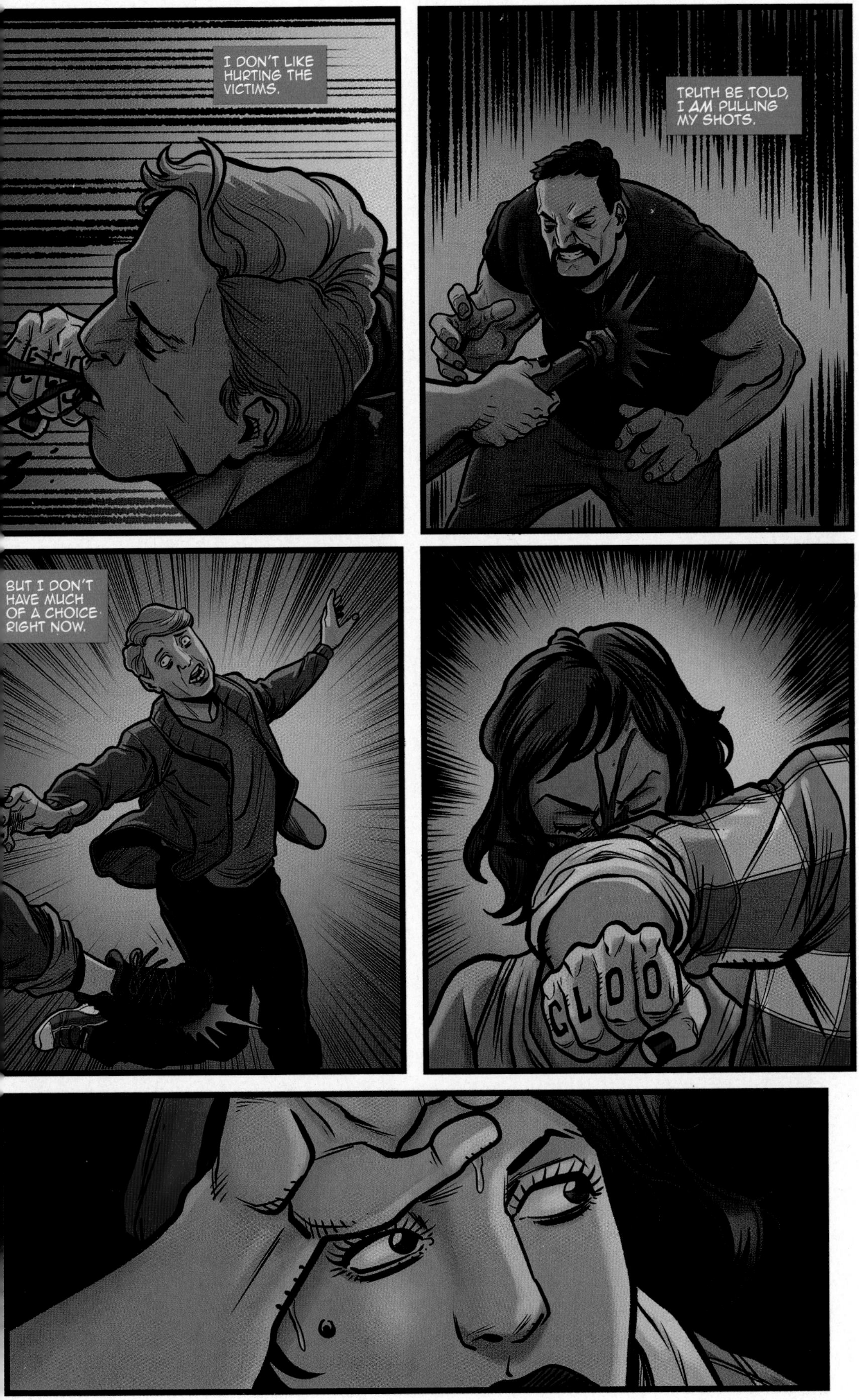
I DON'T LIKE HURTING THE VICTIMS.
TRUTH BE TOLD, I AM PULLING MY SHOTS.
BUT I DON'T HAVE MUCH OF A CHOICE RIGHT NOW.
GLOO

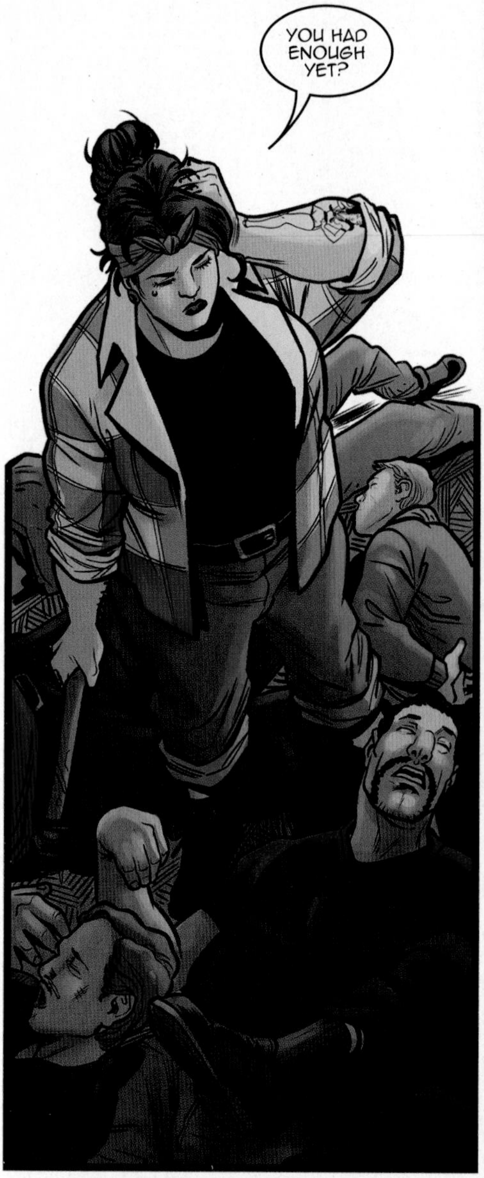
YOU HAD ENOUGH YET?

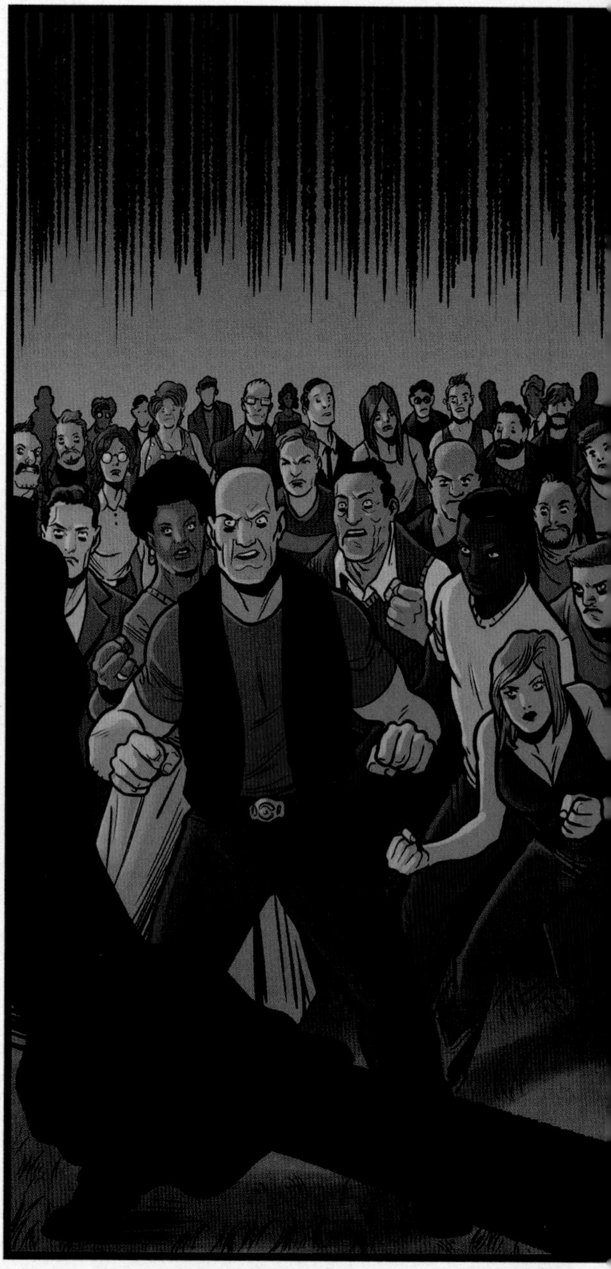

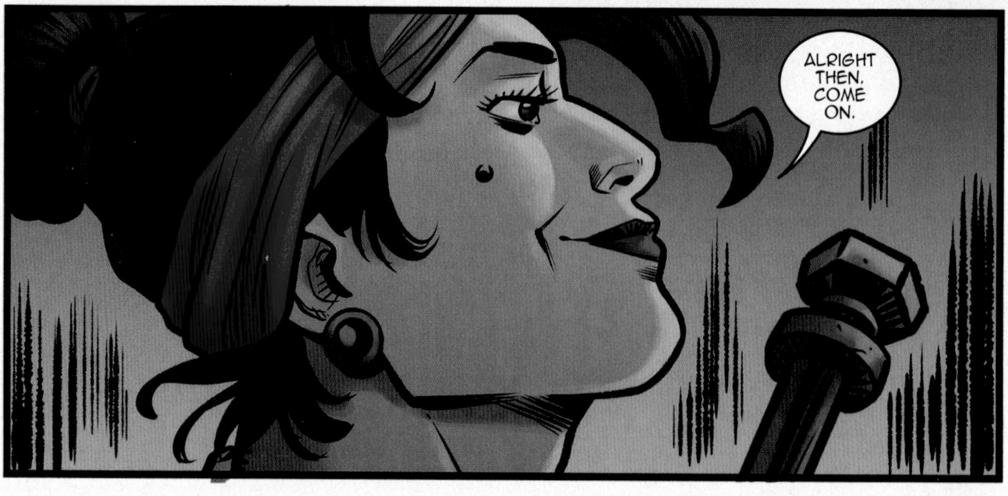
ALRIGHT THEN. COME ON.

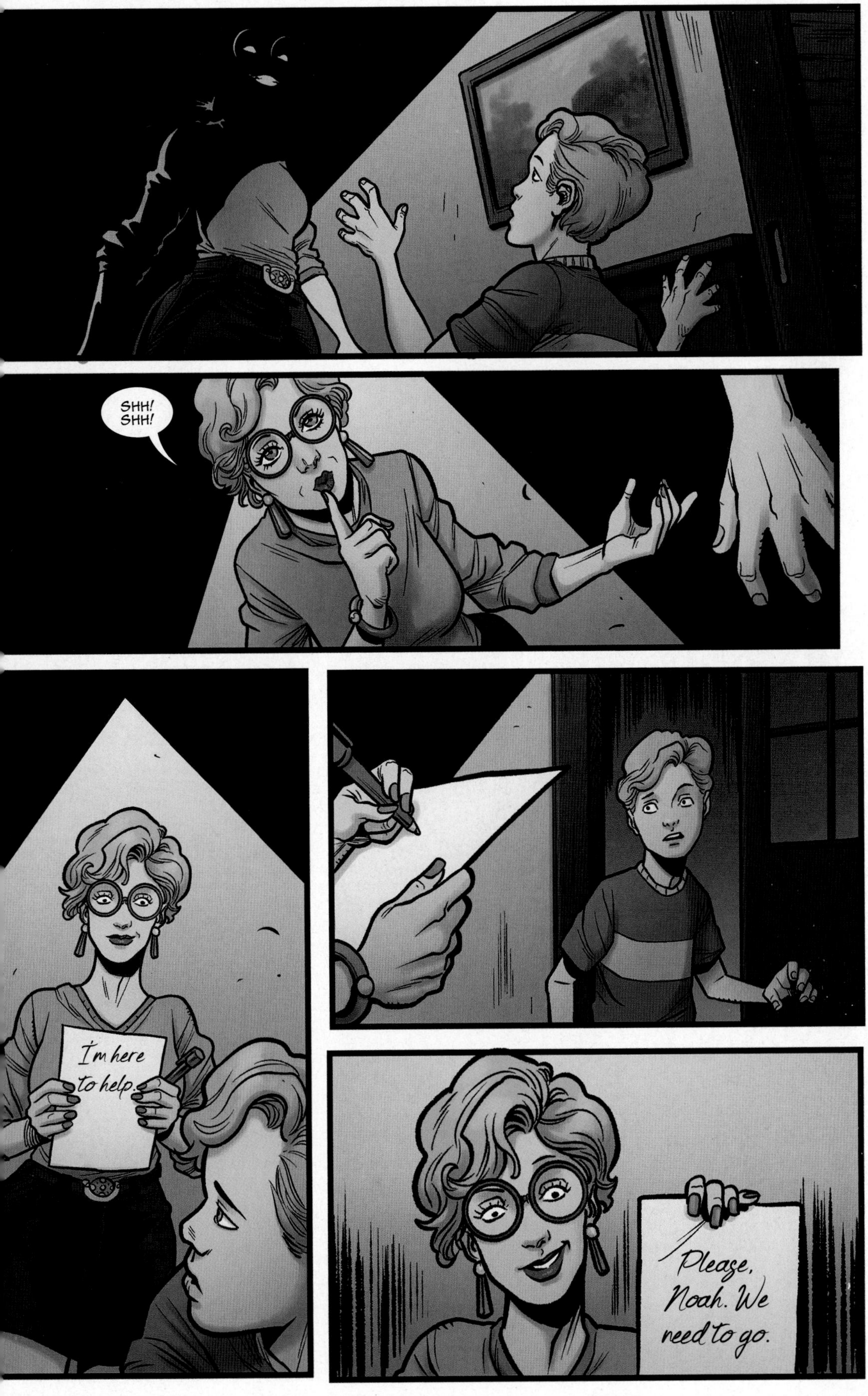
SHH! SHH!
I'm here to help.
Please, Noah. We need to go.

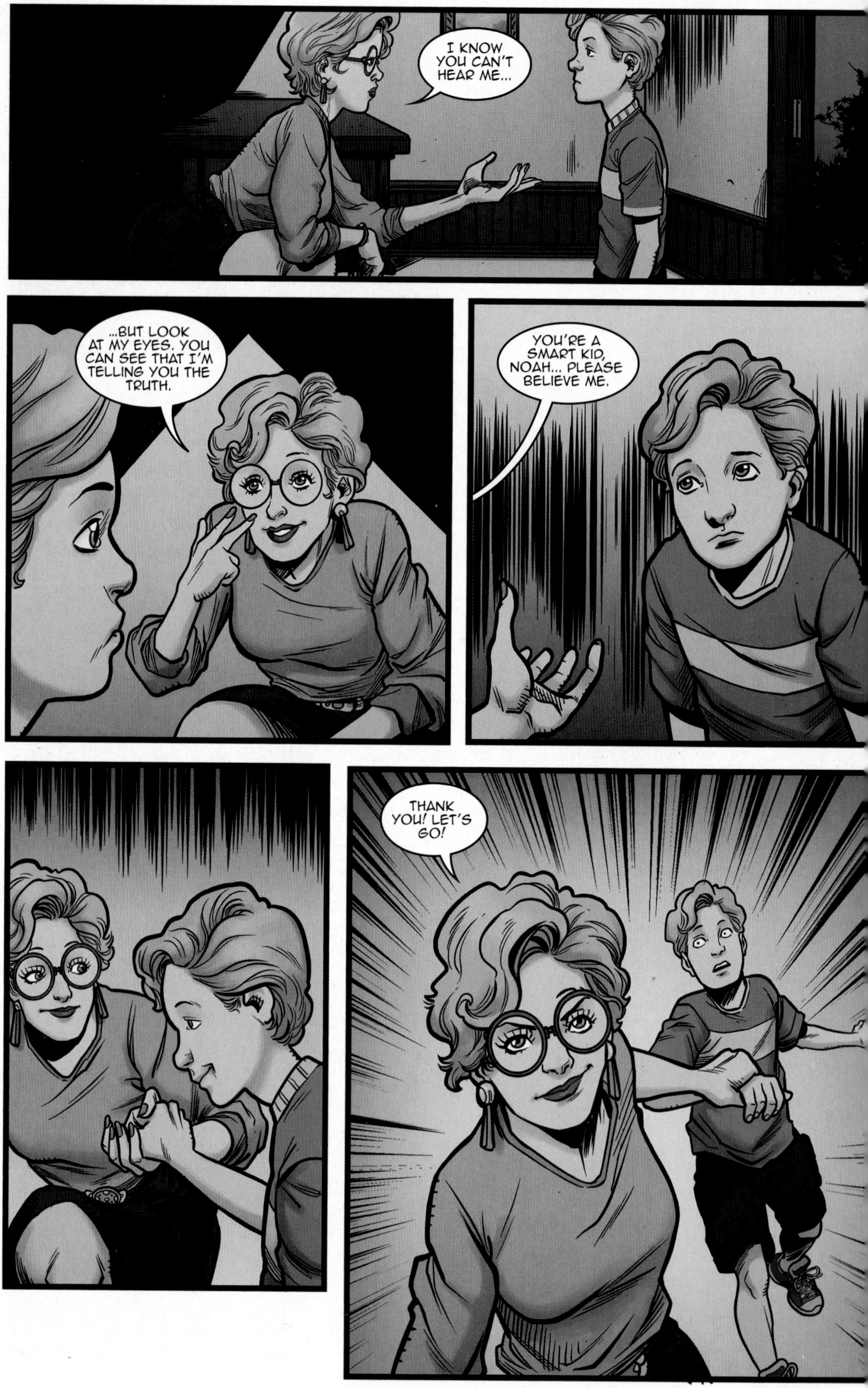
I KNOW YOU CAN'T HEAR ME...
...BUT LOOK AT MY EYES. YOU CAN SEE THAT I'M TELLING YOU THE TRUTH.
YOU'RE A SMART KID, NOAH... PLEASE BELIEVE ME.
THANK YOU! LET'S GO!

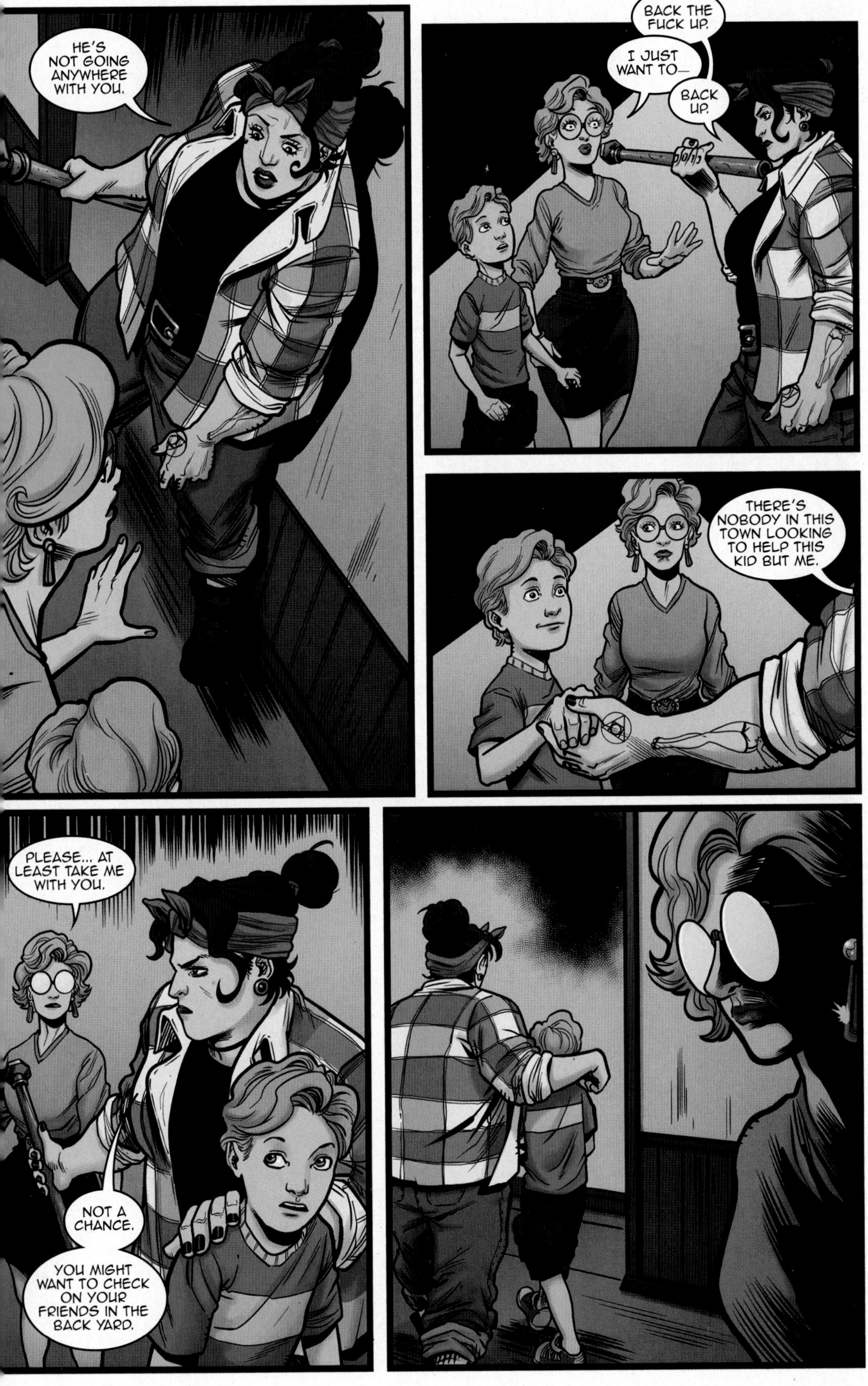
HE'S NOT GOING ANYWHERE WITH YOU.
BACK THE FUCK UP.
I JUST WANT TO—
BACK UP.
THERE'S NOBODY IN THIS TOWN LOOKING TO HELP THIS KID BUT ME.
PLEASE... AT LEAST TAKE ME WITH YOU.
NOT A CHANCE.
YOU MIGHT WANT TO CHECK ON YOUR FRIENDS IN THE BACK YARD.

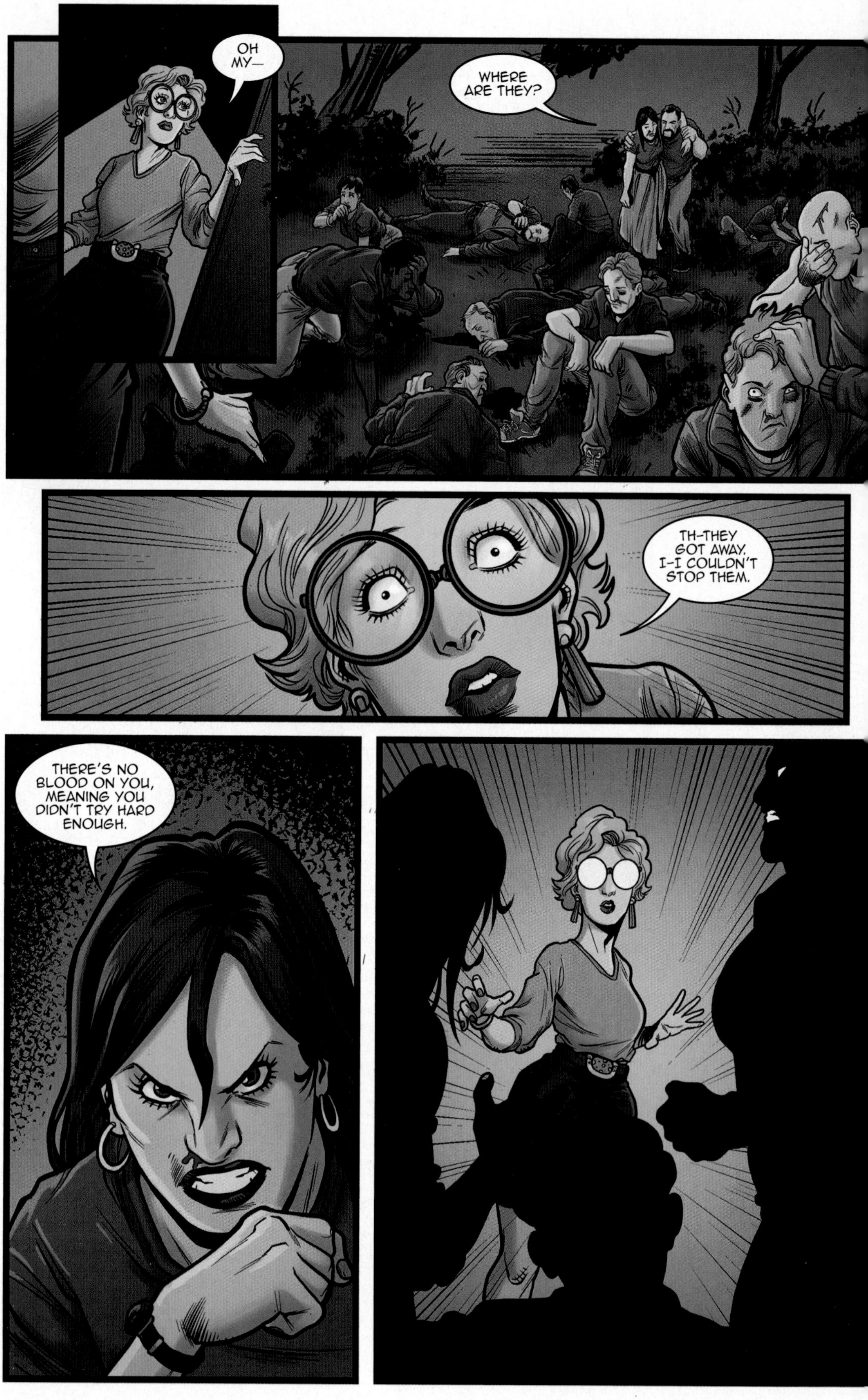
OH MY—
WHERE ARE THEY?
TH—THEY GOT AWAY. I—I COULDN'T STOP THEM.
THERE'S NO BLOOD ON YOU, MEANING YOU DIDN'T TRY HARD ENOUGH.

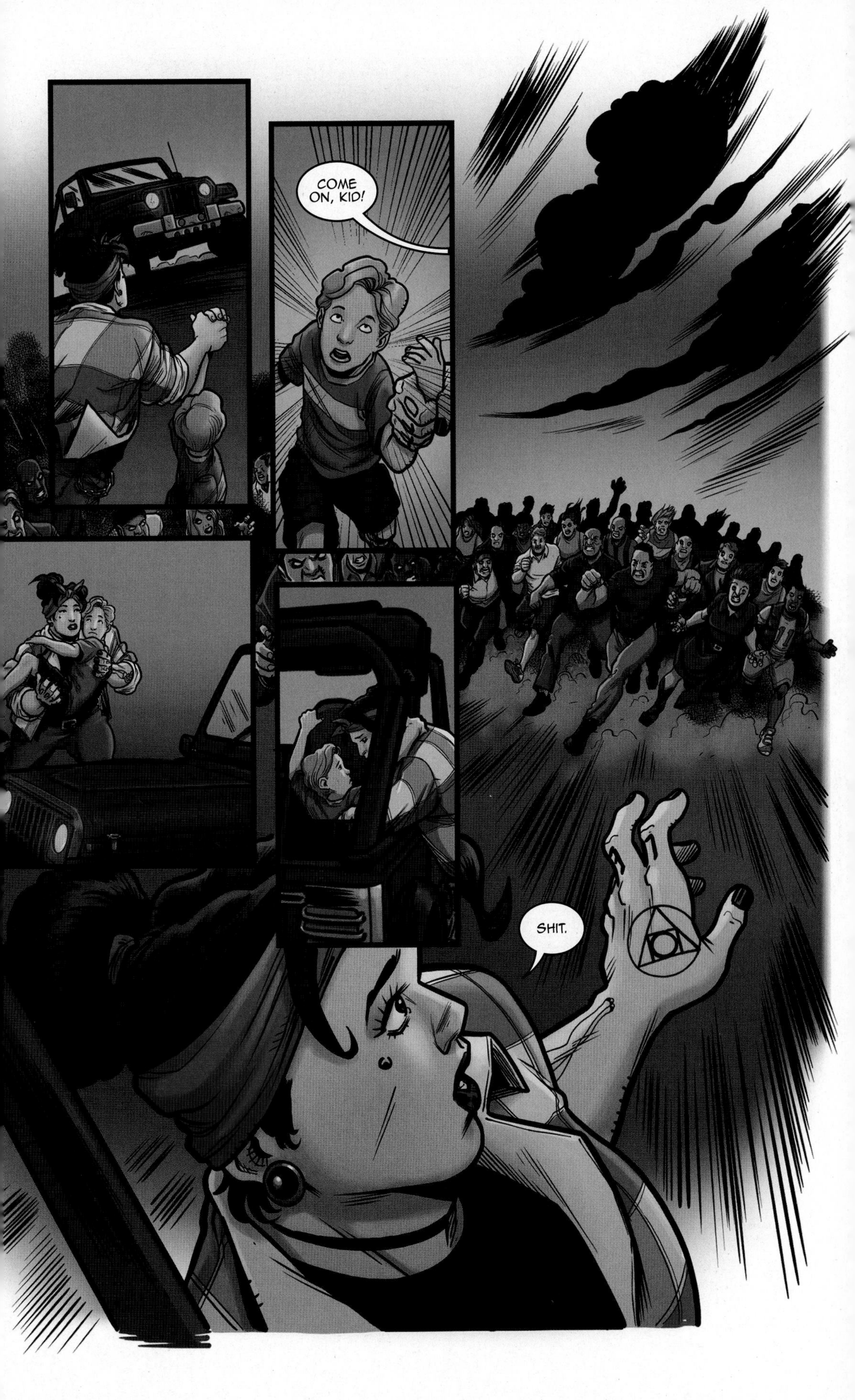
COME ON, KID!
SHIT.

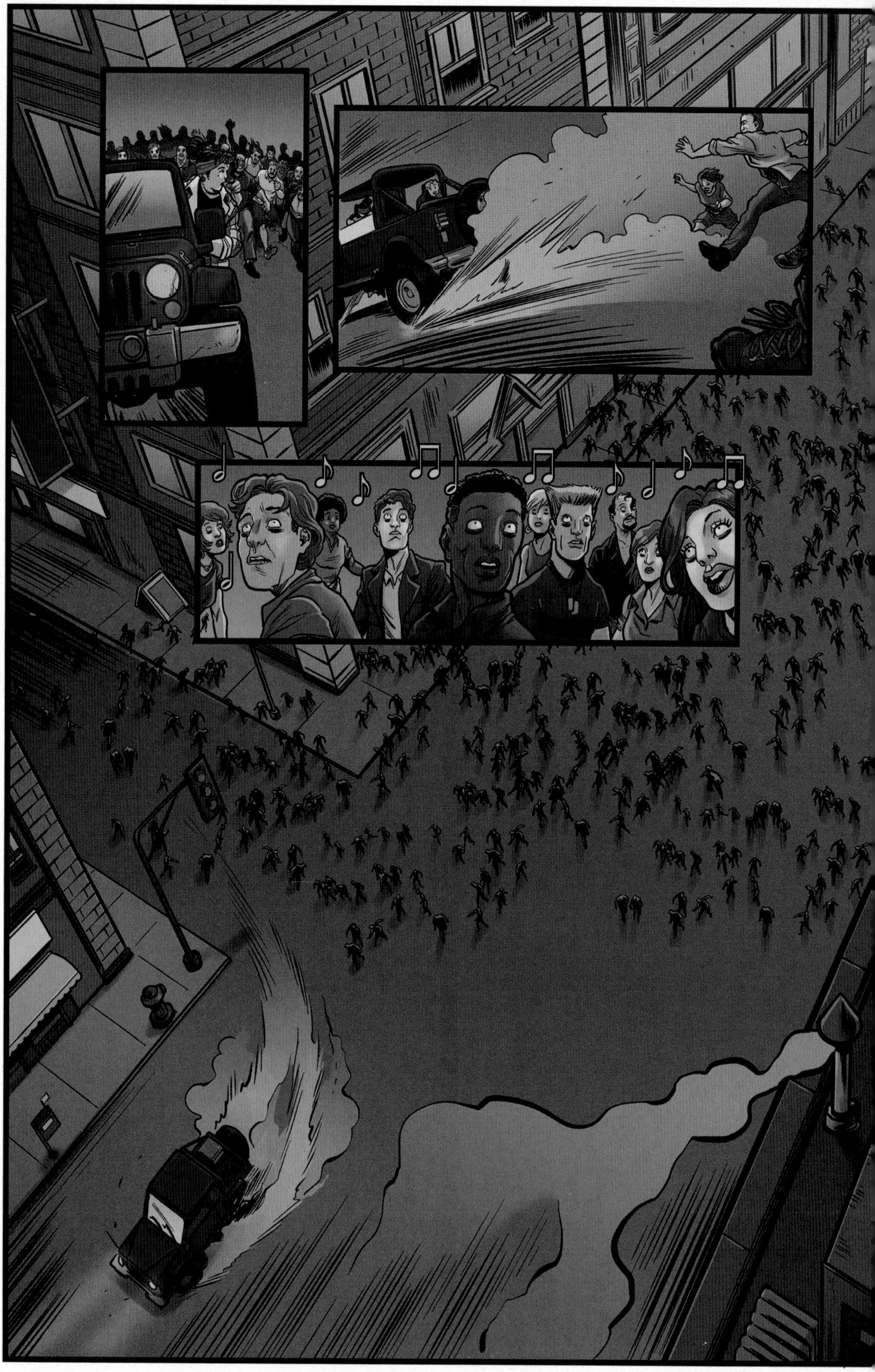

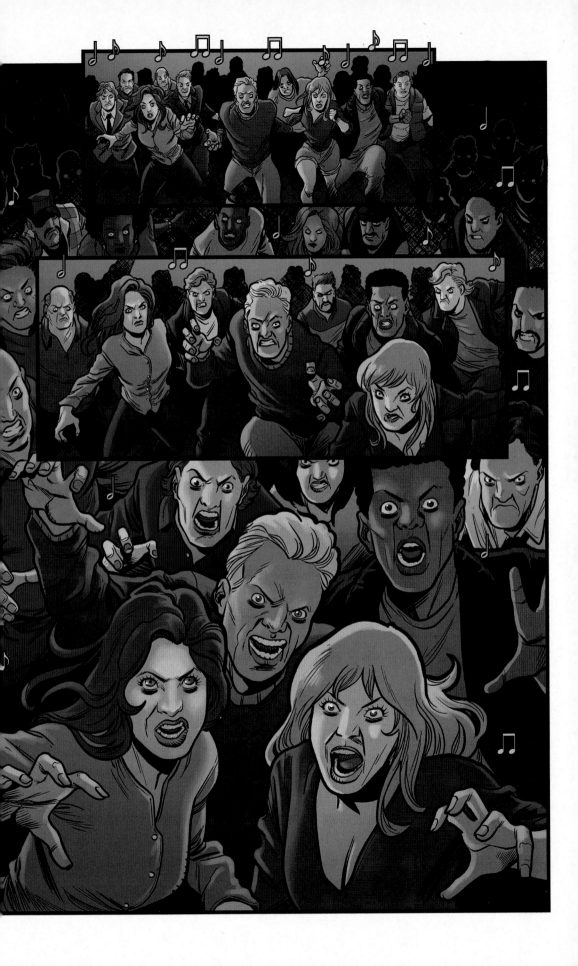

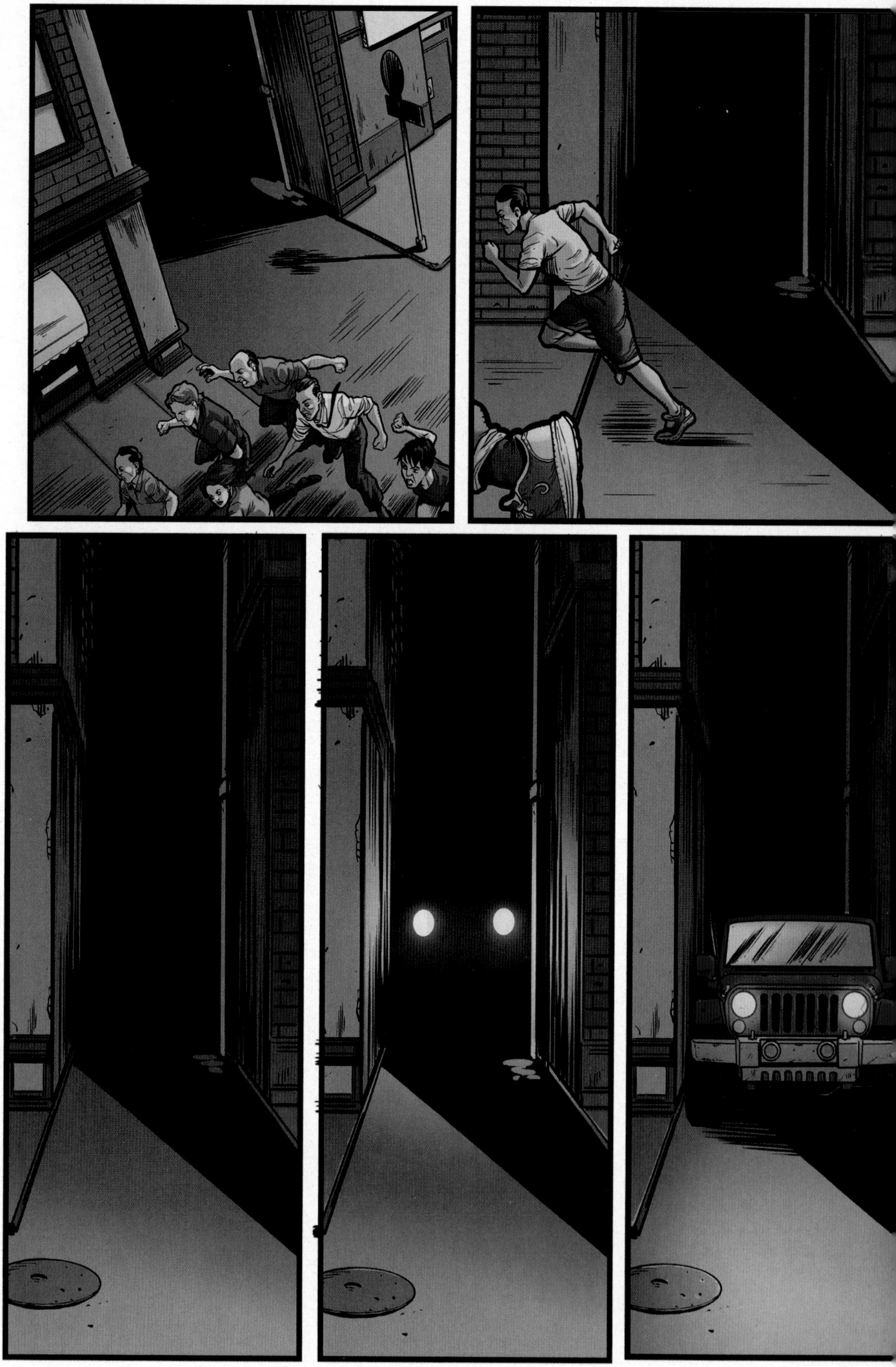

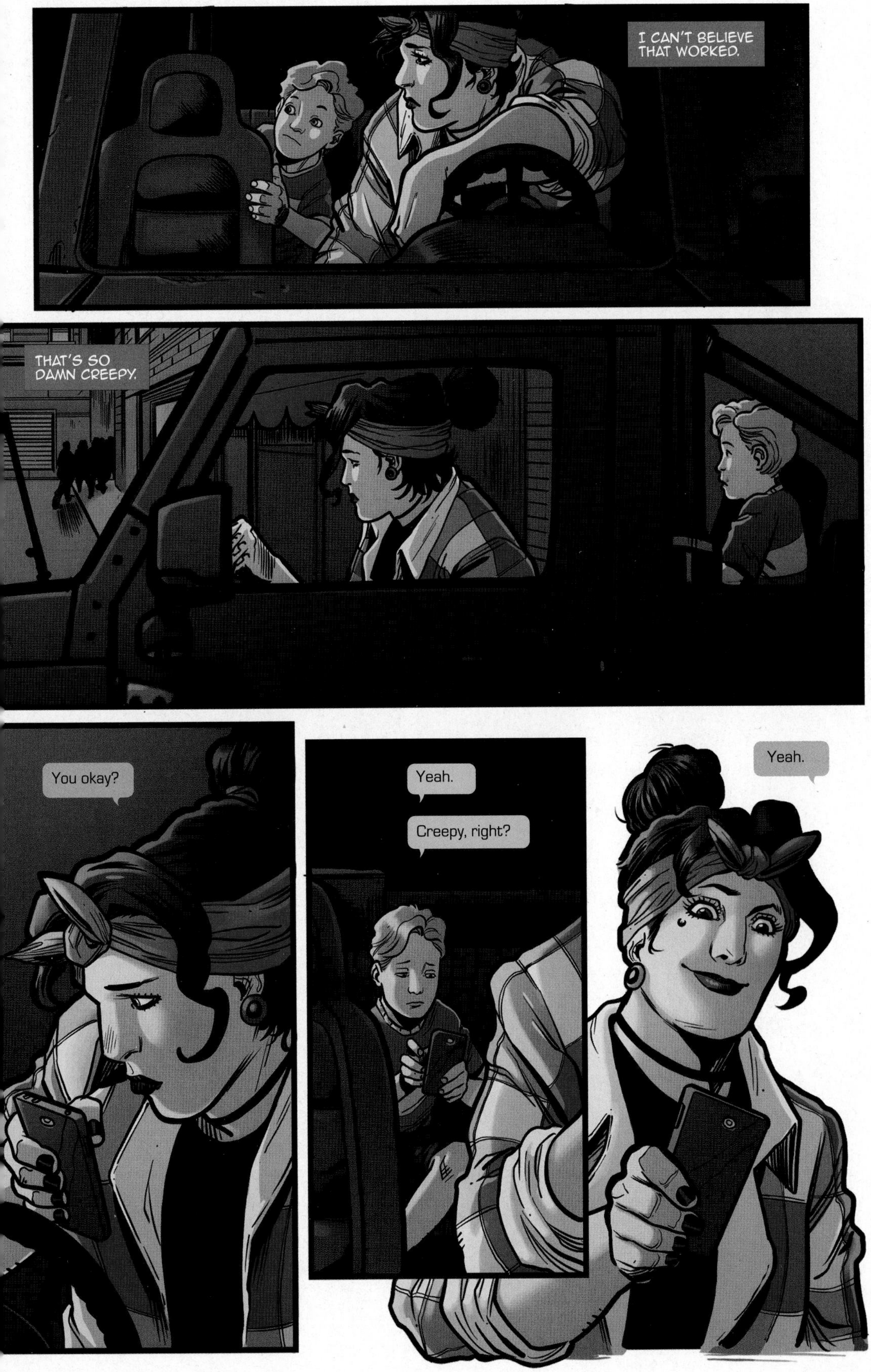
I CAN'T BELIEVE THAT WORKED.
THAT'S SO DAMN CREEPY.
You okay?
Yeah.
Creepy, right?
Yeah.

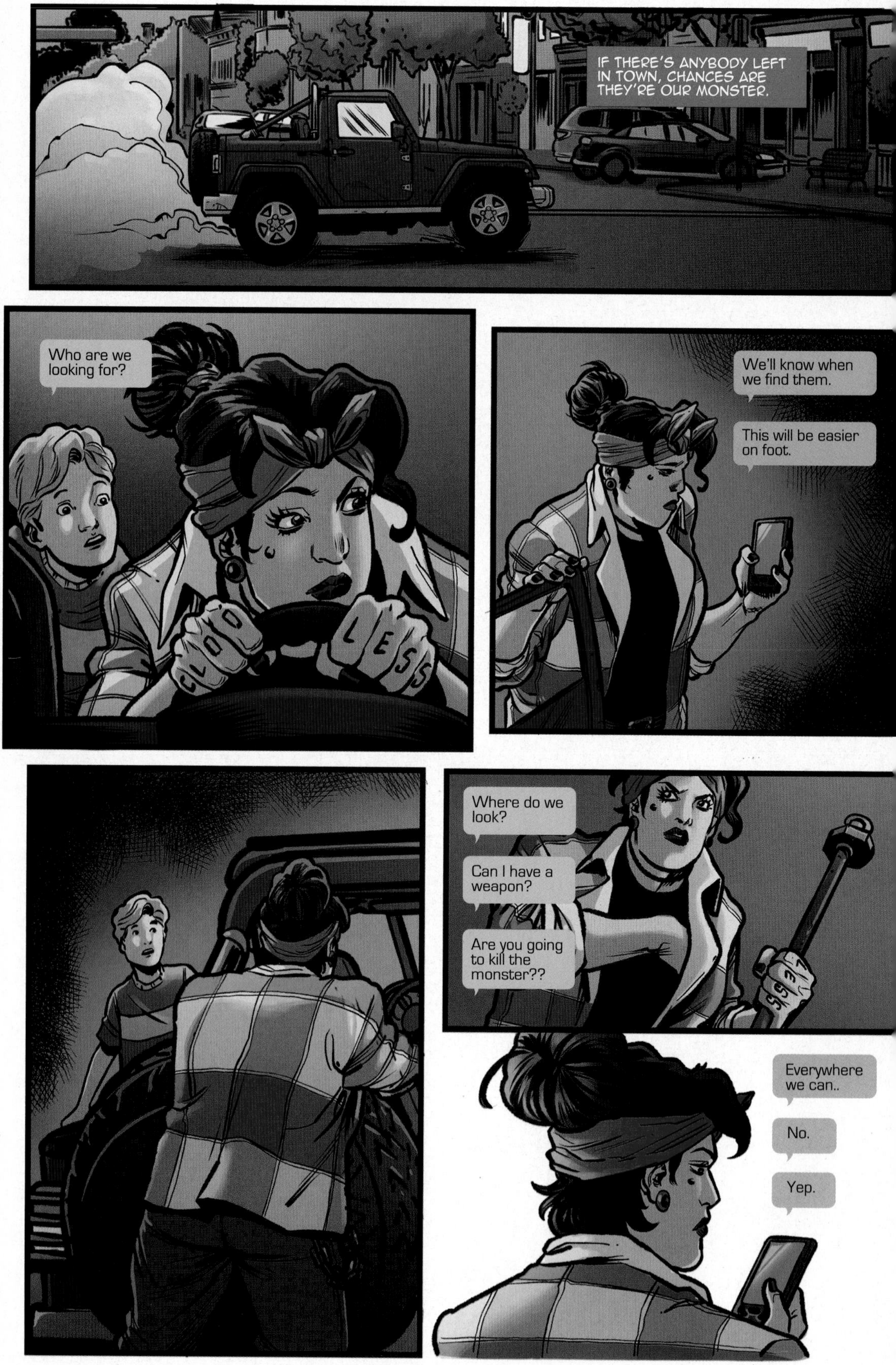
IF THERE'S ANYBODY LEFT IN TOWN, CHANCES ARE THEY'RE OUR MONSTER.
Who are we looking for?
CLODLESS
We'll know when we find them.
This will be easier on foot.
Where do we look?
Can I have a weapon?
Are you going to kill the monster??
Everywhere we can..
No.
Yep.

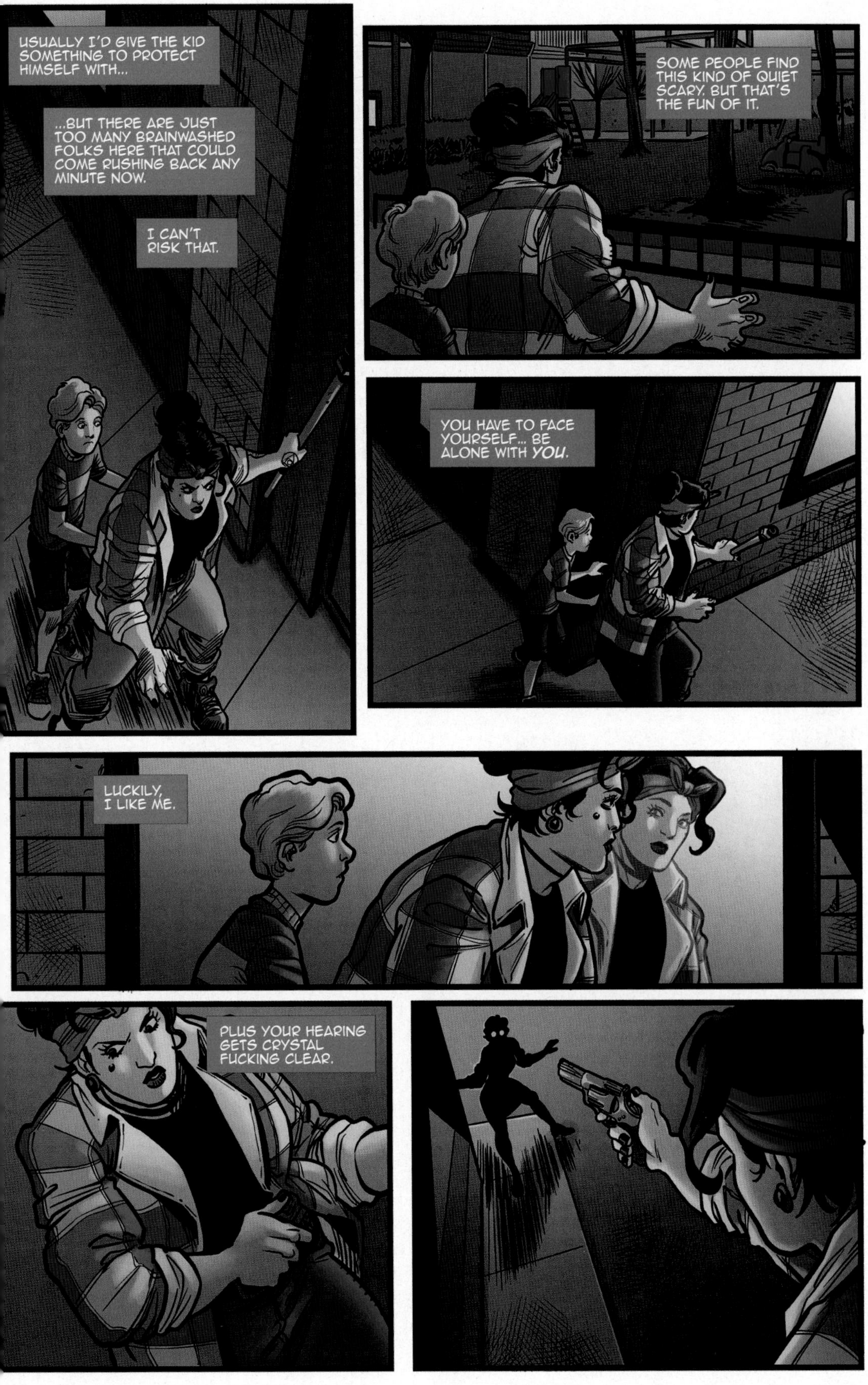
USUALLY I'D GIVE THE KID SOMETHING TO PROTECT HIMSELF WITH...
...BUT THERE ARE JUST TOO MANY BRAINWASHED FOLKS HERE THAT COULD COME RUSHING BACK ANY MINUTE NOW.
I CAN'T RISK THAT.
SOME PEOPLE FIND THIS KIND OF QUIET SCARY. BUT THAT'S THE FUN OF IT.
YOU HAVE TO FACE YOURSELF... BE ALONE WITH *YOU*.
LUCKILY, I LIKE ME.
PLUS YOUR HEARING GETS CRYSTAL FUCKING CLEAR.

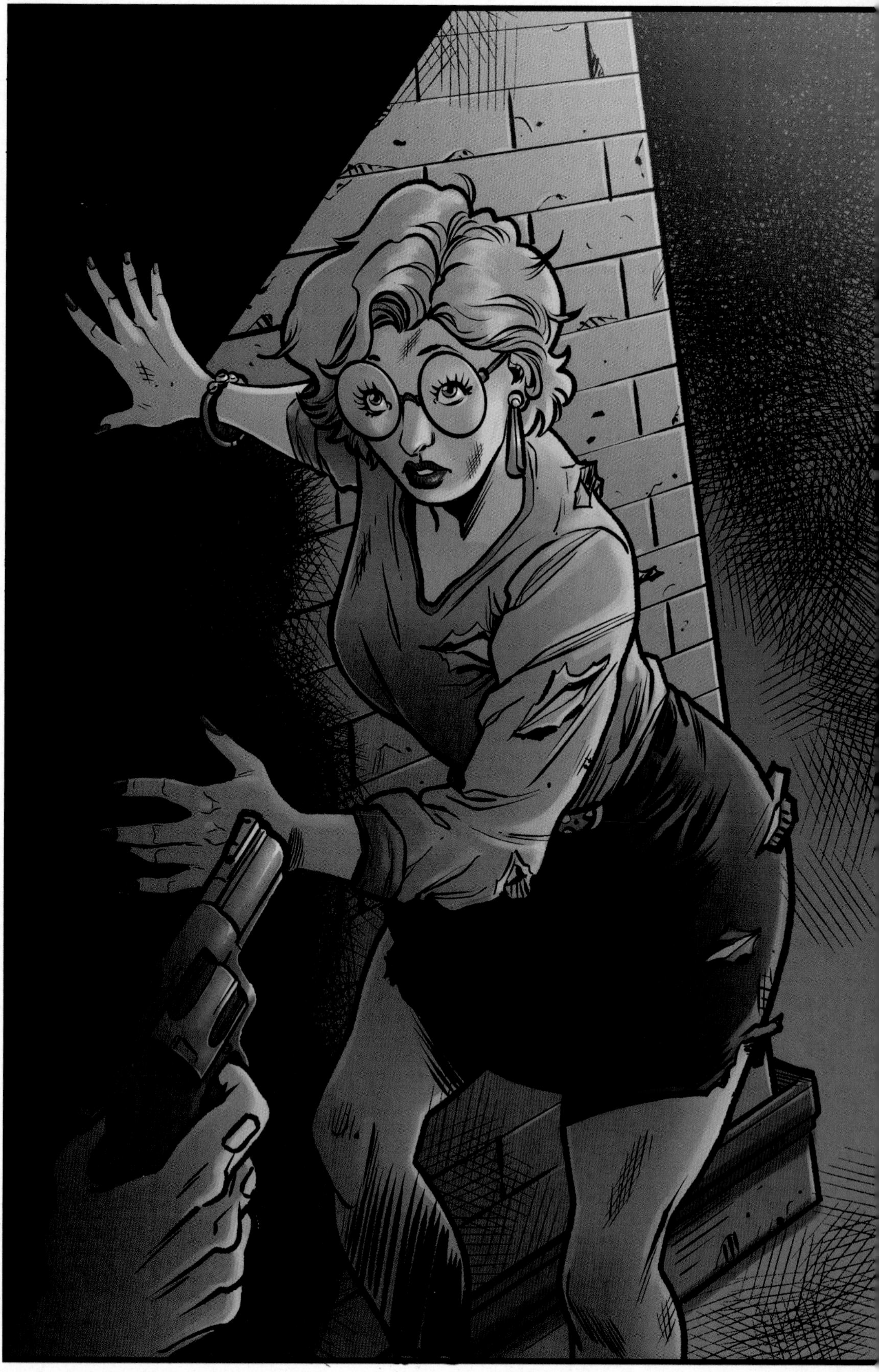

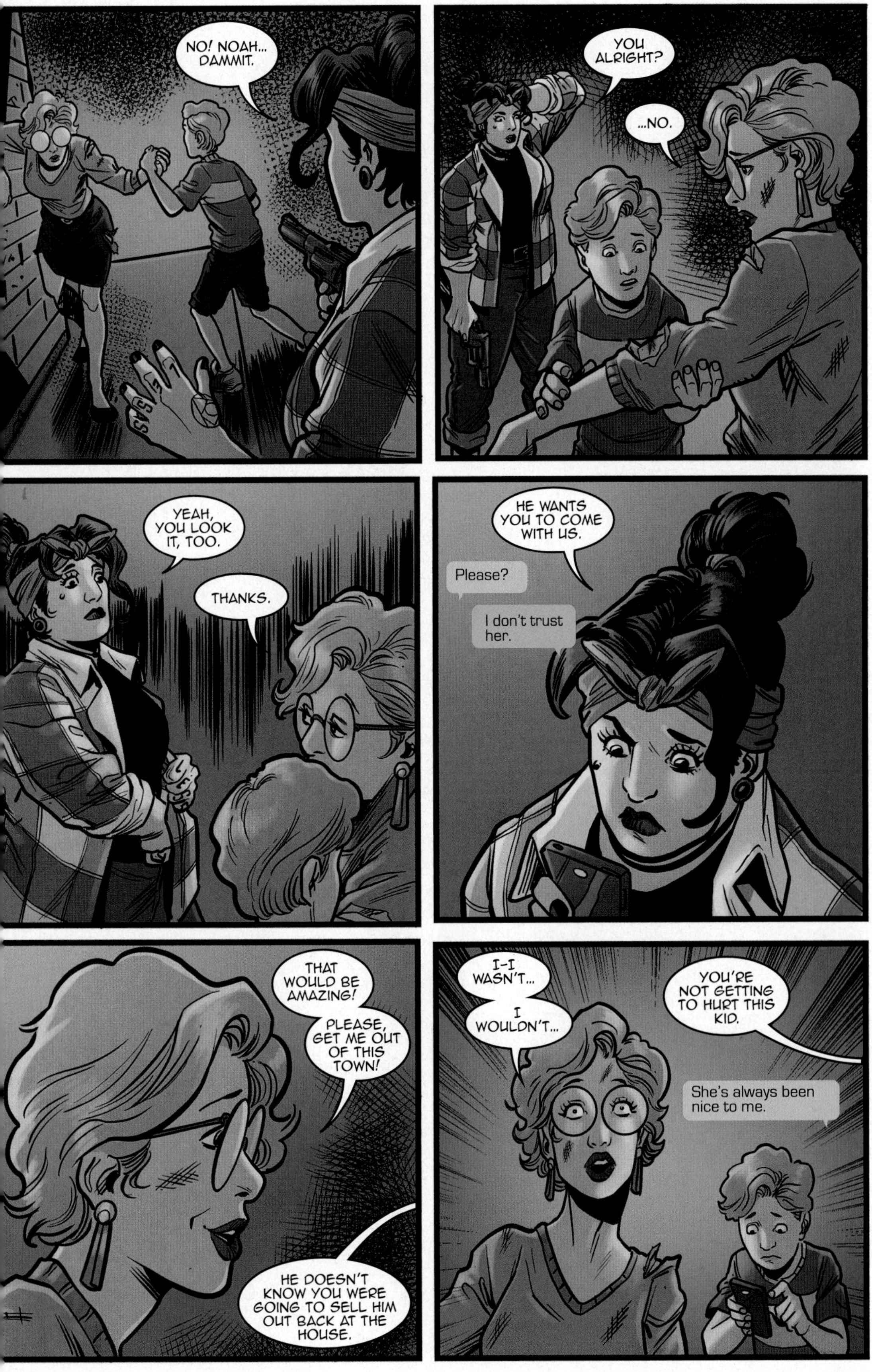
NO! NOAH... DAMMIT.
YOU ALRIGHT?
...NO.
YEAH, YOU LOOK IT, TOO.
THANKS.
HE WANTS YOU TO COME WITH US.
Please?
I don't trust her.
THAT WOULD BE AMAZING!
PLEASE, GET ME OUT OF THIS TOWN!
HE DOESN'T KNOW YOU WERE GOING TO SELL HIM OUT BACK AT THE HOUSE.
I-I WASN'T...
I WOULDN'T...
YOU'RE NOT GETTING TO HURT THIS KID.
She's always been nice to me.

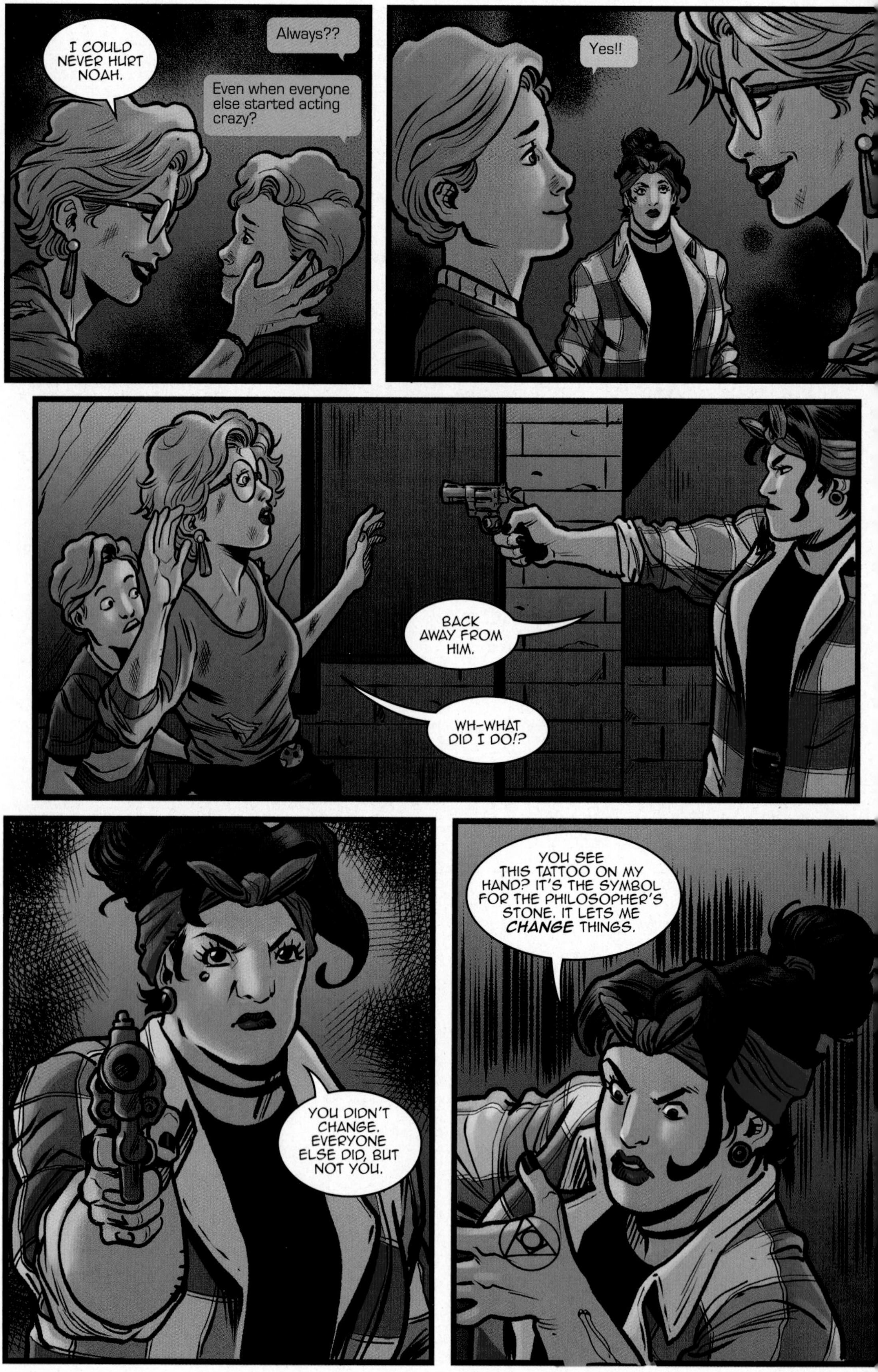

I COULD NEVER HURT NOAH.
Always??
Even when everyone else started acting crazy?
Yes!!
BACK AWAY FROM HIM.
WH-WHAT DID I DO!?
YOU DIDN'T CHANGE. EVERYONE ELSE DID, BUT NOT YOU.
YOU SEE THIS TATTOO ON MY HAND? IT'S THE SYMBOL FOR THE PHILOSOPHER'S STONE. IT LETS ME *CHANGE* THINGS.

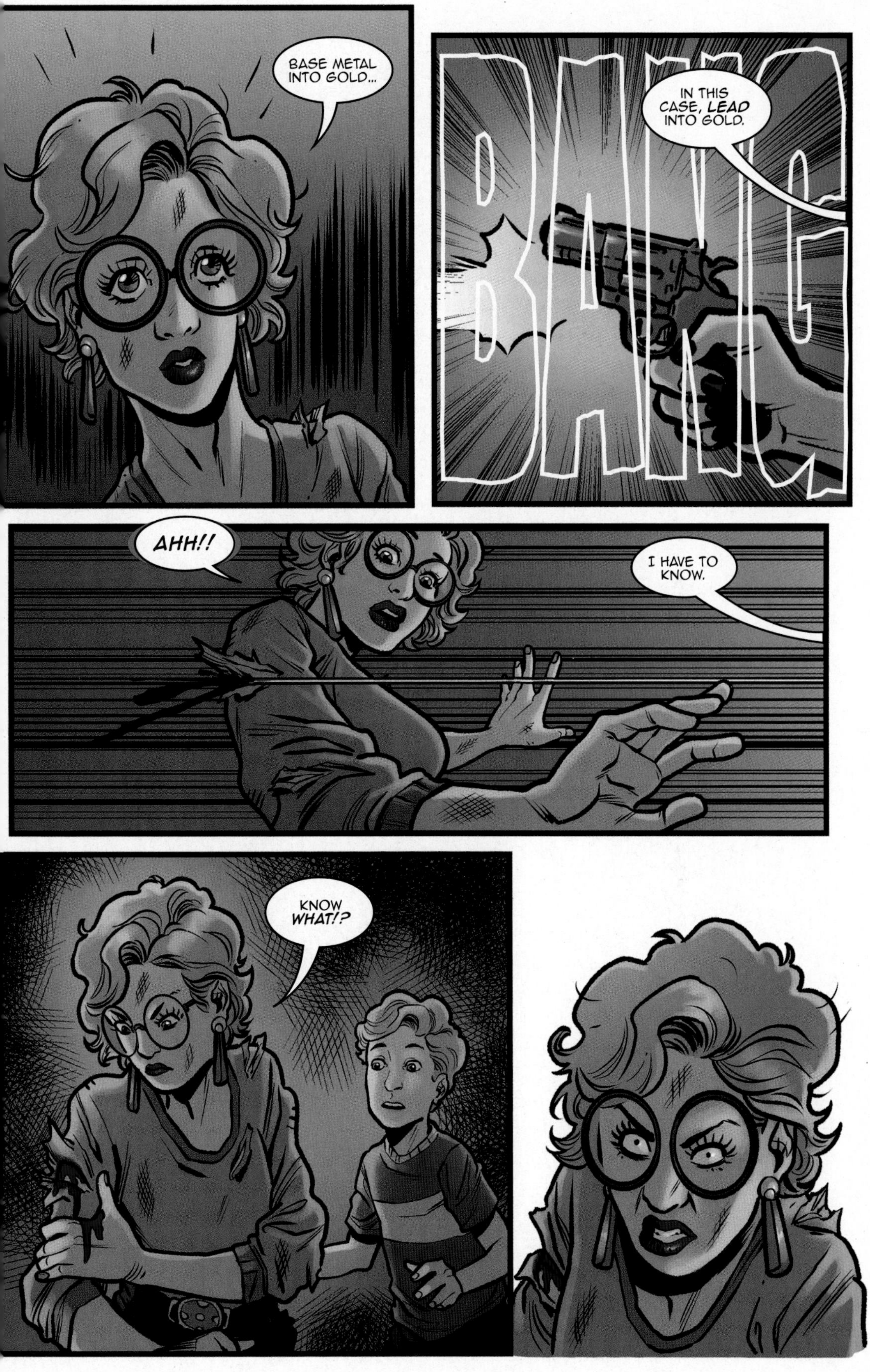
BASE METAL INTO GOLD...
BANG
IN THIS CASE, LEAD INTO GOLD.
AHH!!
I HAVE TO KNOW.
KNOW WHAT!?

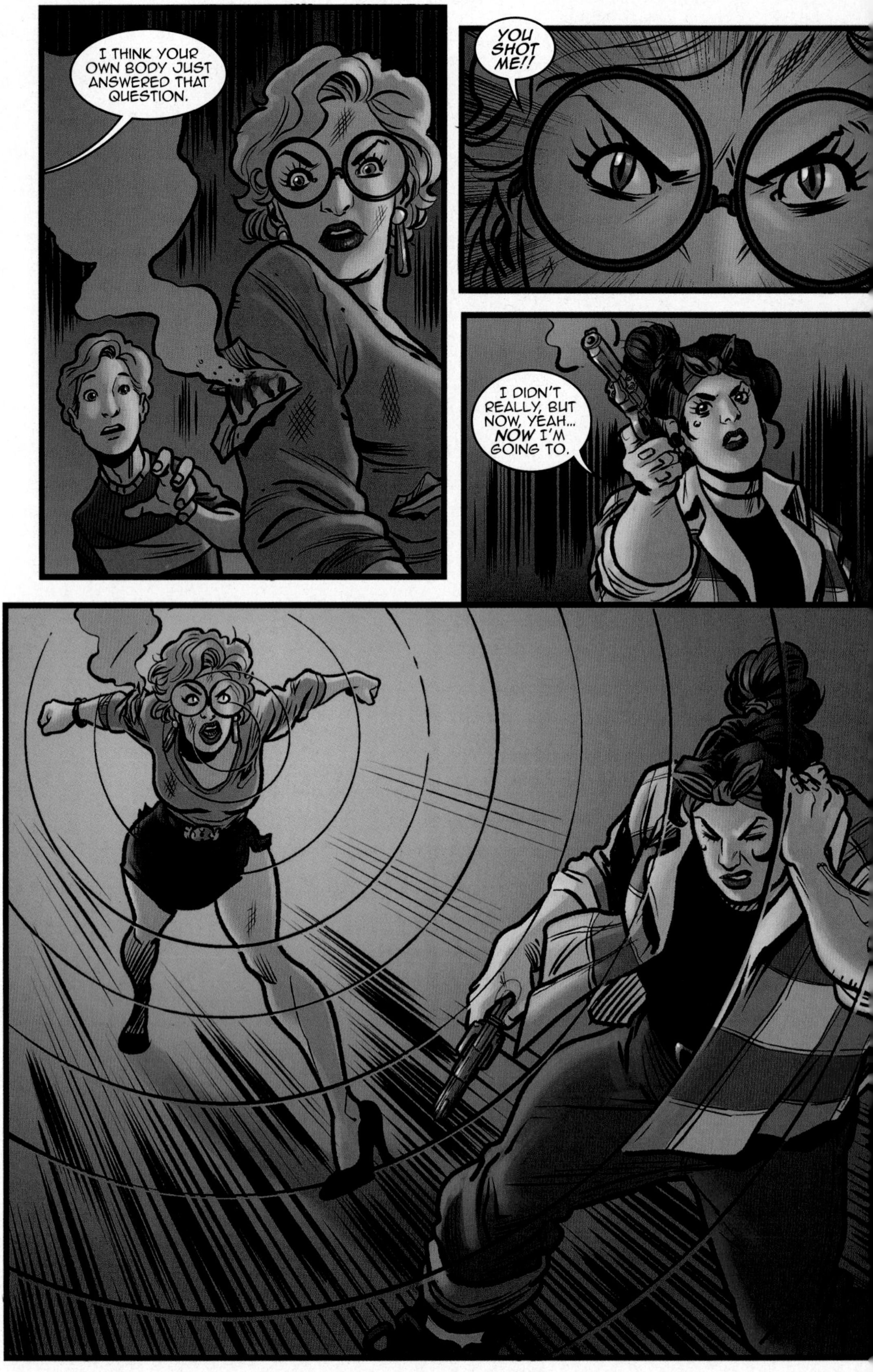
I THINK YOUR OWN BODY JUST ANSWERED THAT QUESTION.
YOU SHOT ME!!
I DIDN'T REALLY, BUT NOW, YEAH... *NOW* I'M GOING TO.

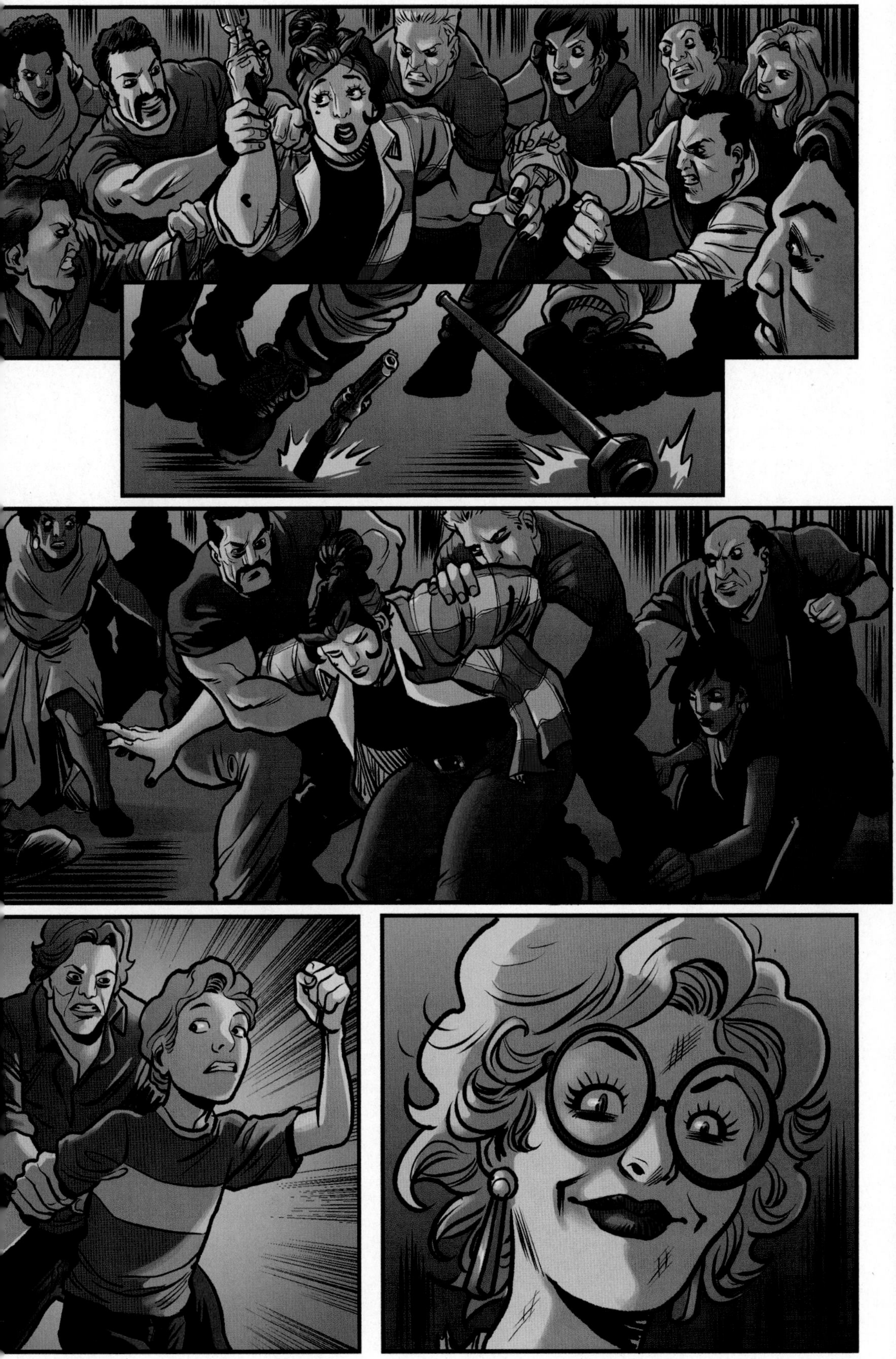

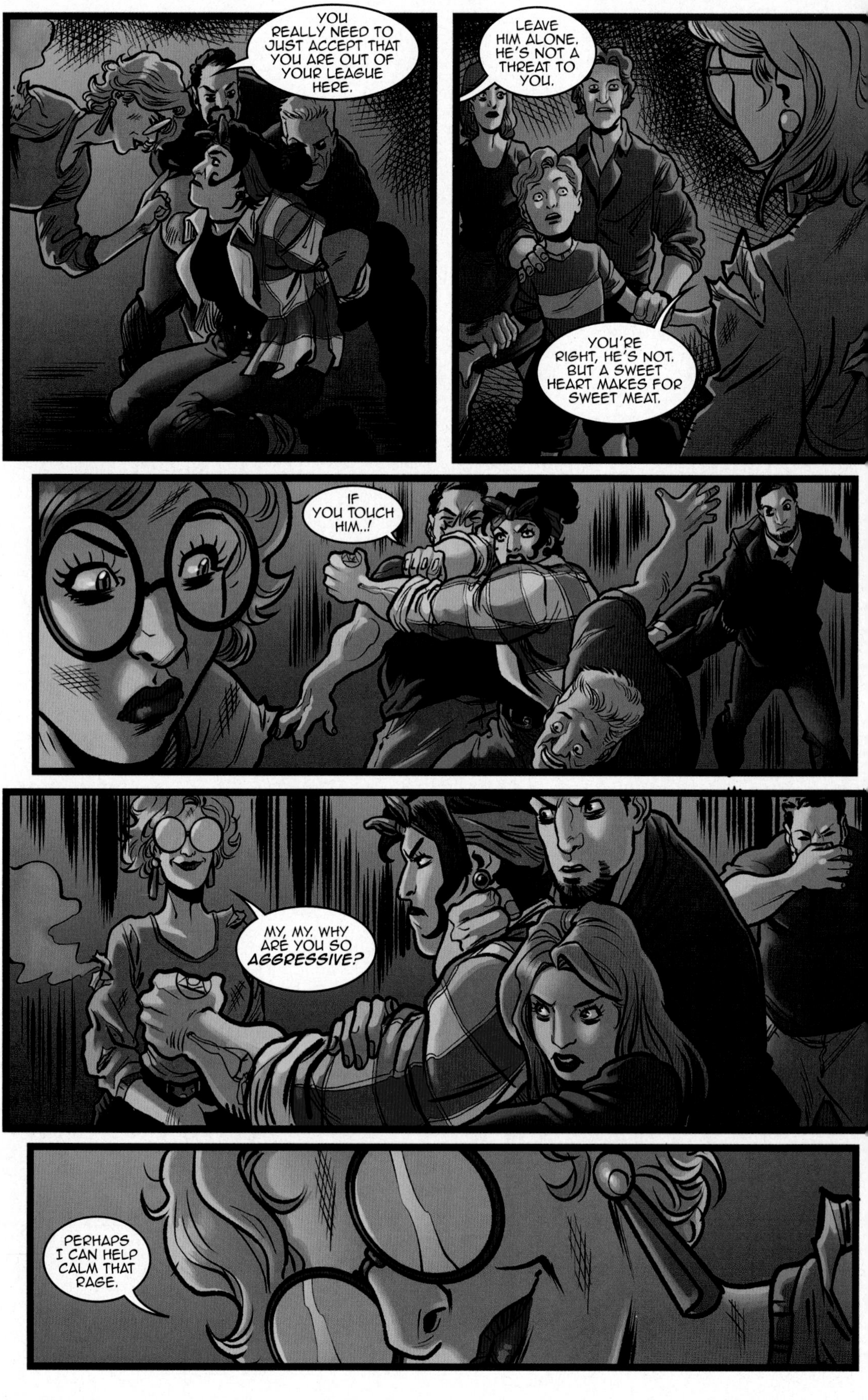
YOU REALLY NEED TO JUST ACCEPT THAT YOU ARE OUT OF YOUR LEAGUE HERE.
LEAVE HIM ALONE. HE'S NOT A THREAT TO YOU.
YOU'RE RIGHT, HE'S NOT. BUT A SWEET HEART MAKES FOR SWEET MEAT.
IF YOU TOUCH HIM..!
MY, MY. WHY ARE YOU SO *AGGRESSIVE?*
PERHAPS I CAN HELP CALM THAT RAGE.

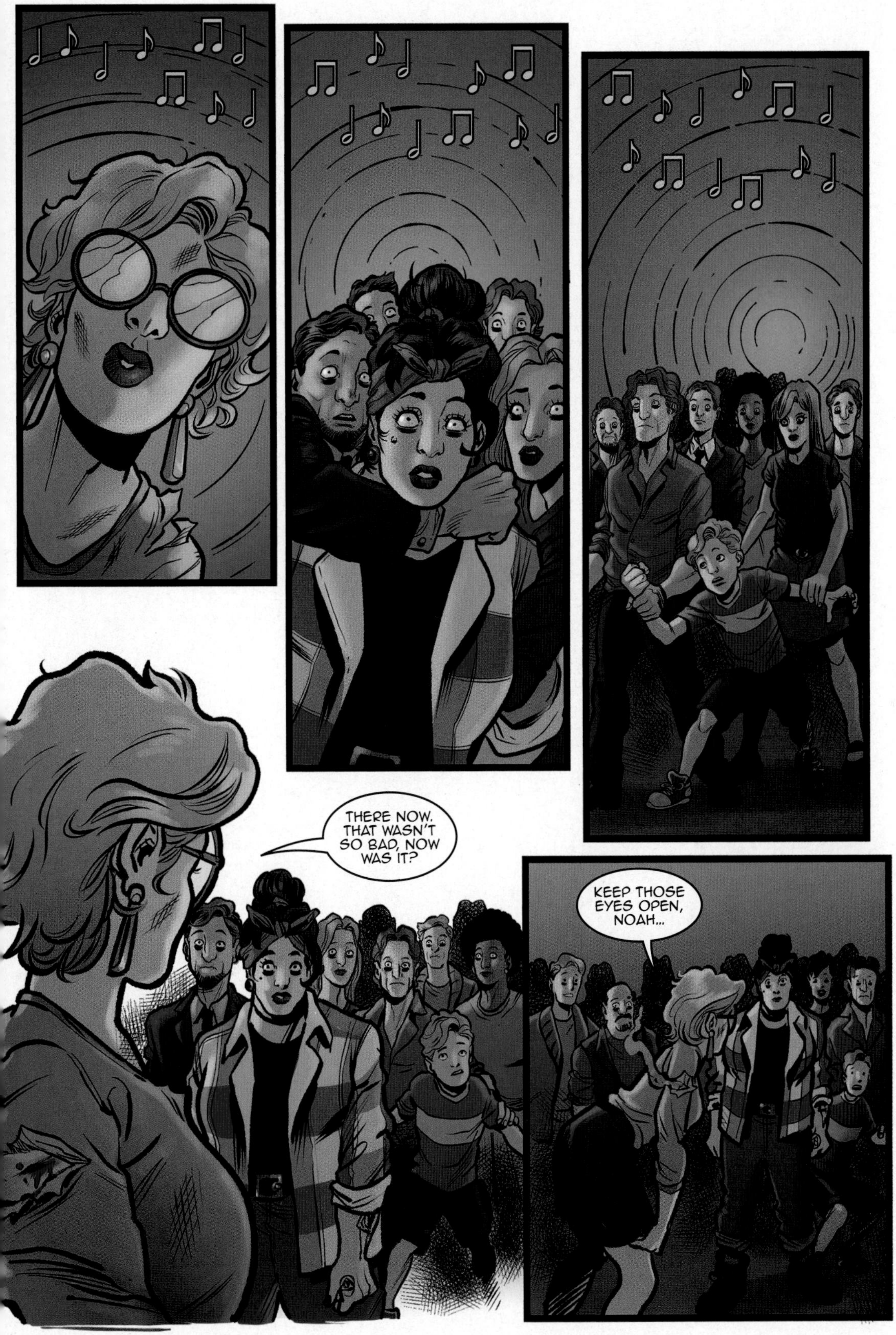
THERE NOW. THAT WASN'T SO BAD, NOW WAS IT?
KEEP THOSE EYES OPEN, NOAH...

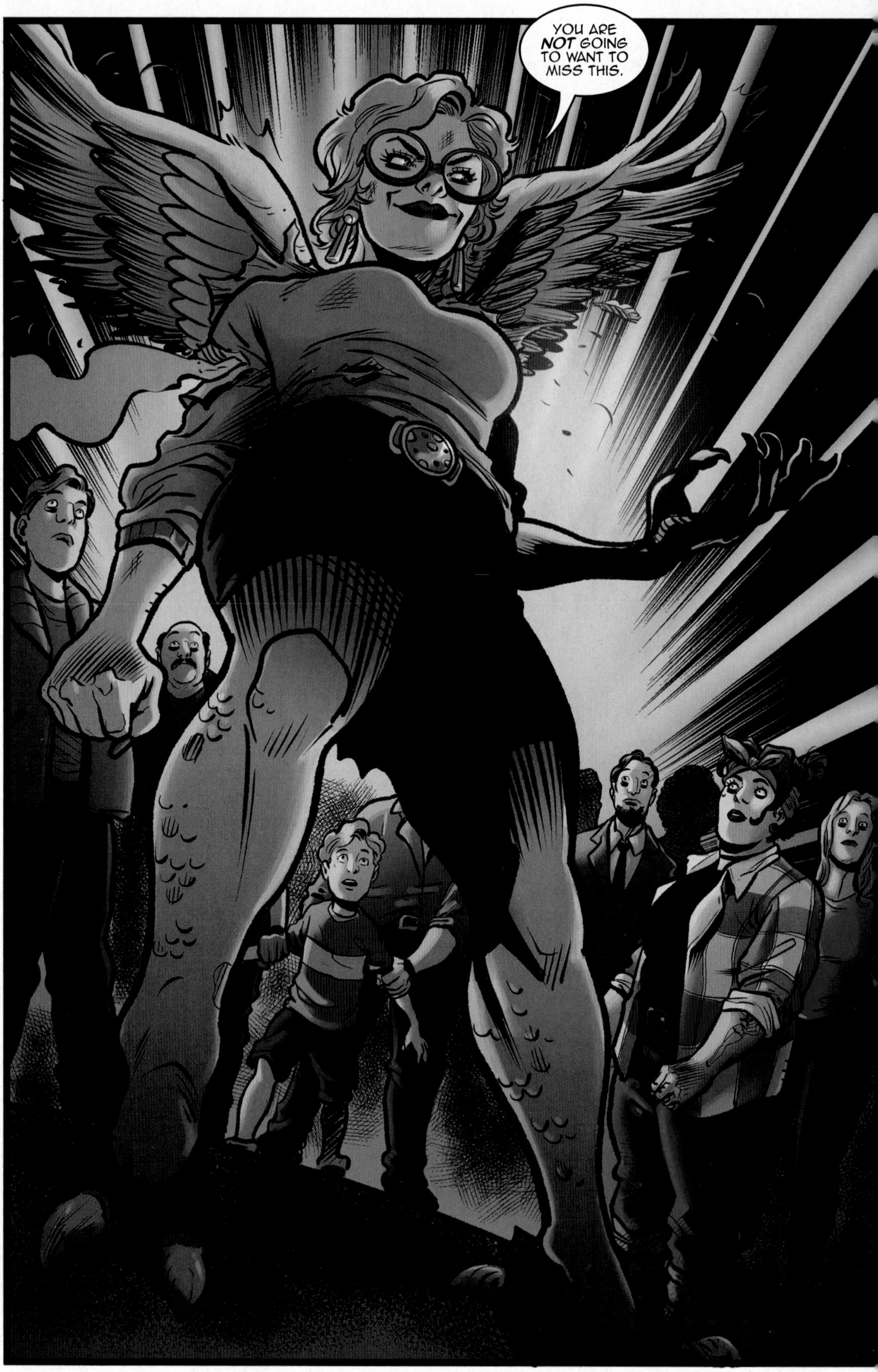
YOU ARE **NOT** GOING TO WANT TO MISS THIS.

MUSICAL INTERLUDE

CHAPTER FOUR

WRITTEN BY
SHAWN GABBORIN

ART BY
RAFAEL DANTAS

COLORS BY
ROSA "ROSAKAZ" RANTILA

SPECIAL THANKS TO DANIEL J. LOGAN

COVERS A & B
RAFAEL DANTAS

COVERS C & D
ANN ULAND

COVERS E & F
BILL MCKAY

Jason Martin: Publisher
Shawn Gabborin: Editor in Chief
Nicole D'Andria: Marketing Director/Editor
Jessica Lowrie: Social Media Czar
Danielle Davison: Executive Administrator
Shawn Pryor: President of Creator Relations
Bryan Seaton: CEO

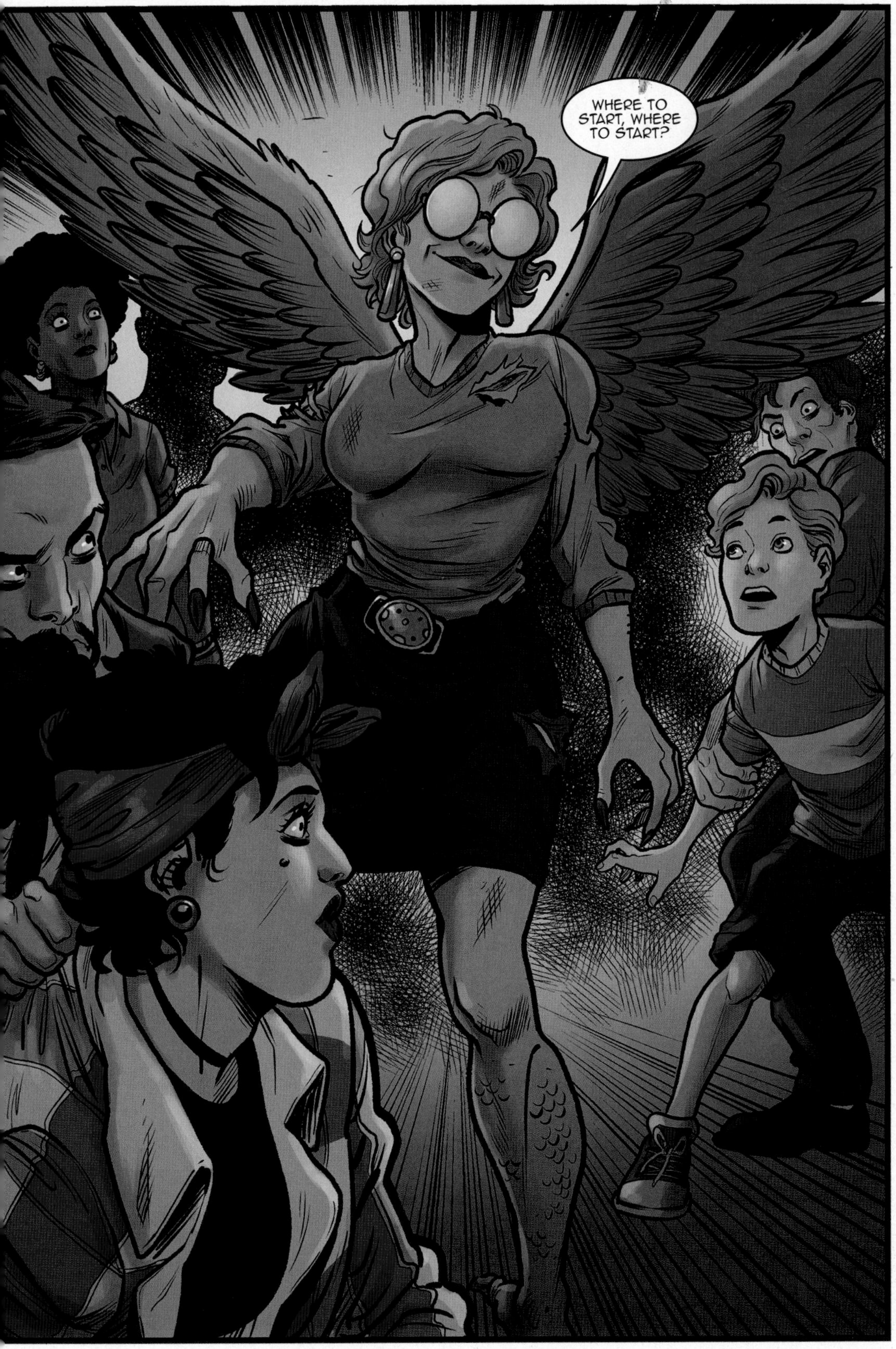
WHERE TO START, WHERE TO START?

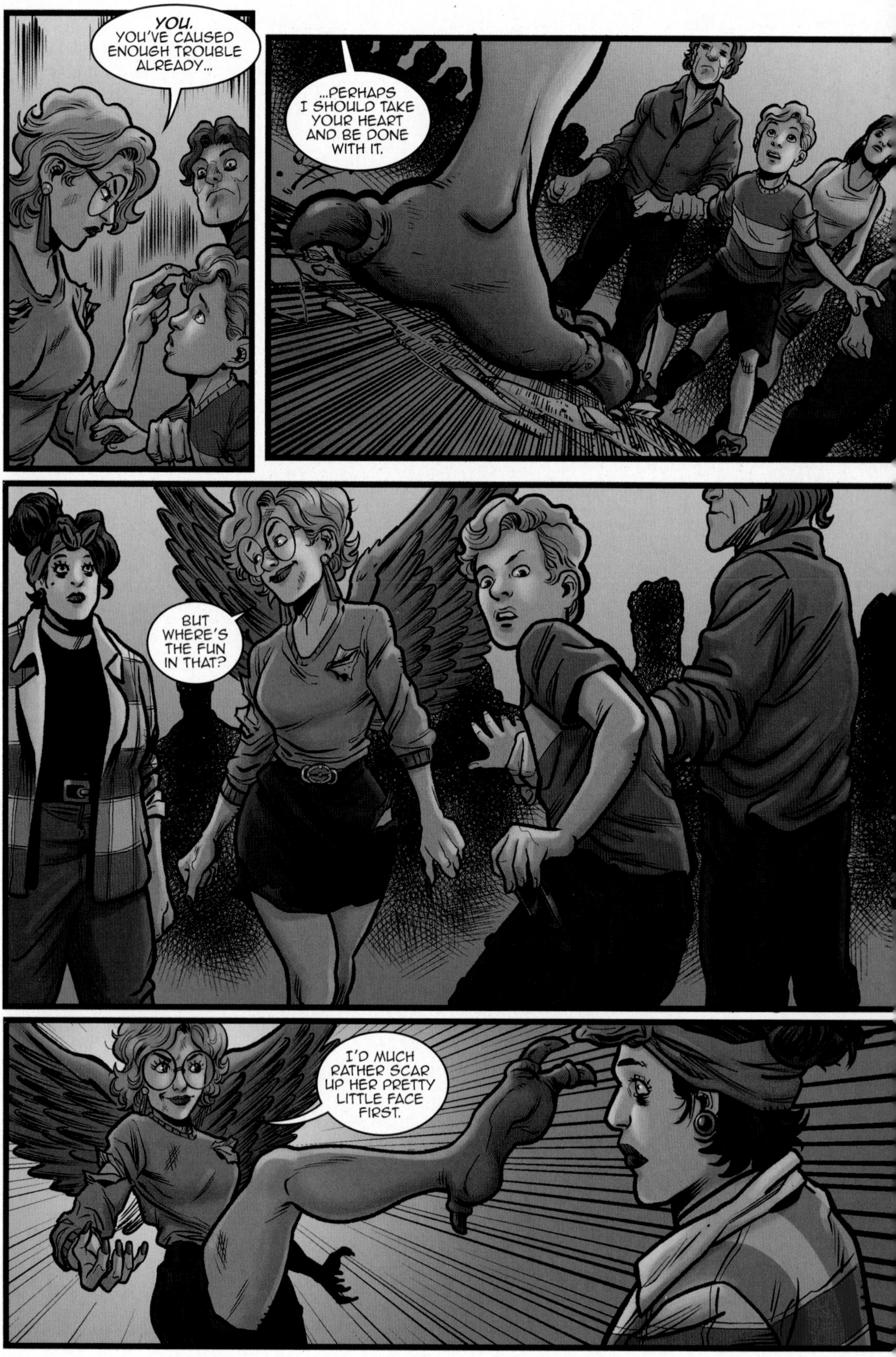
YOU. YOU'VE CAUSED ENOUGH TROUBLE ALREADY...
...PERHAPS I SHOULD TAKE YOUR HEART AND BE DONE WITH IT.
BUT WHERE'S THE FUN IN THAT?
I'D MUCH RATHER SCAR UP HER PRETTY LITTLE FACE FIRST.

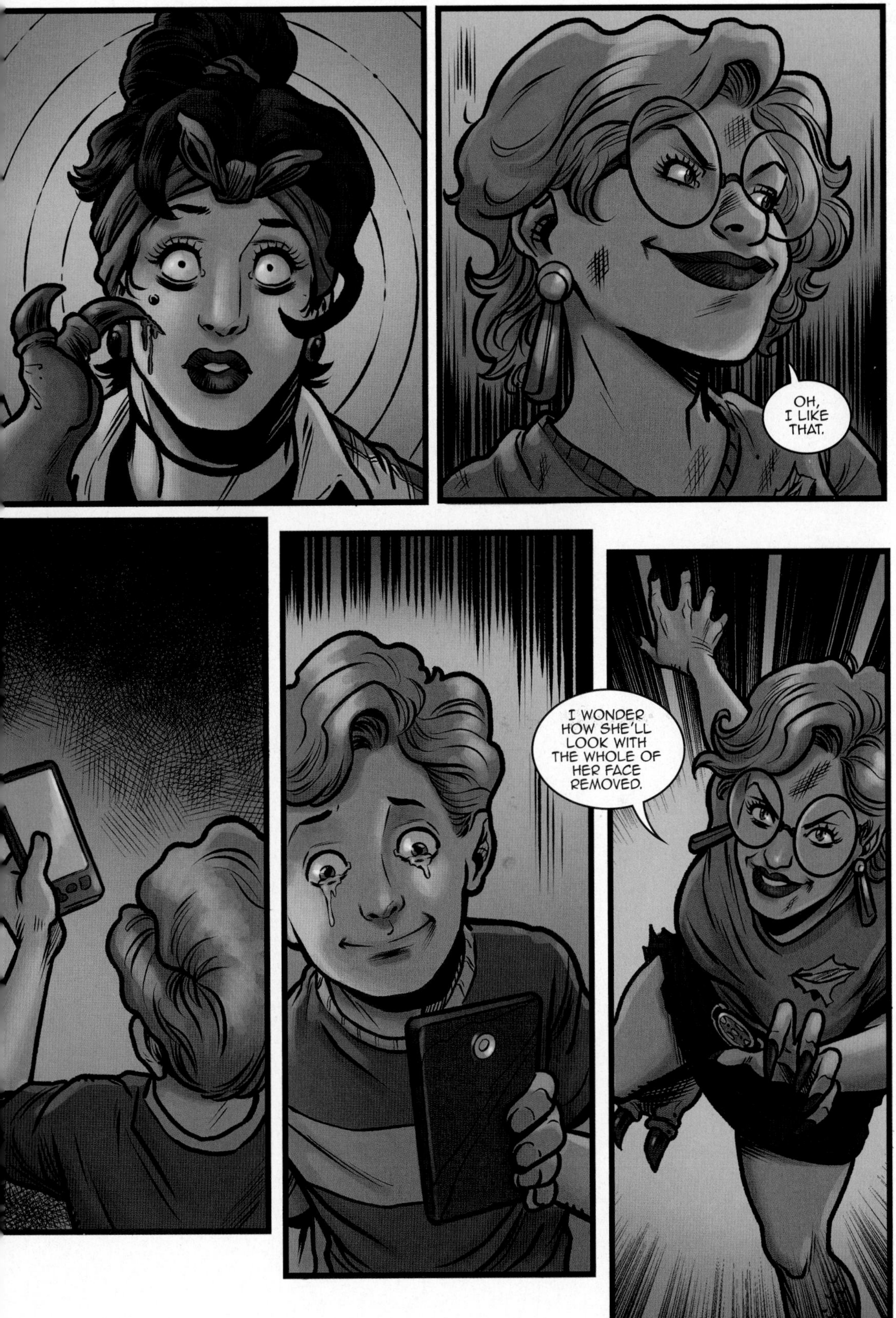
OH, I LIKE THAT.
I WONDER HOW SHE'LL LOOK WITH THE WHOLE OF HER FACE REMOVED.

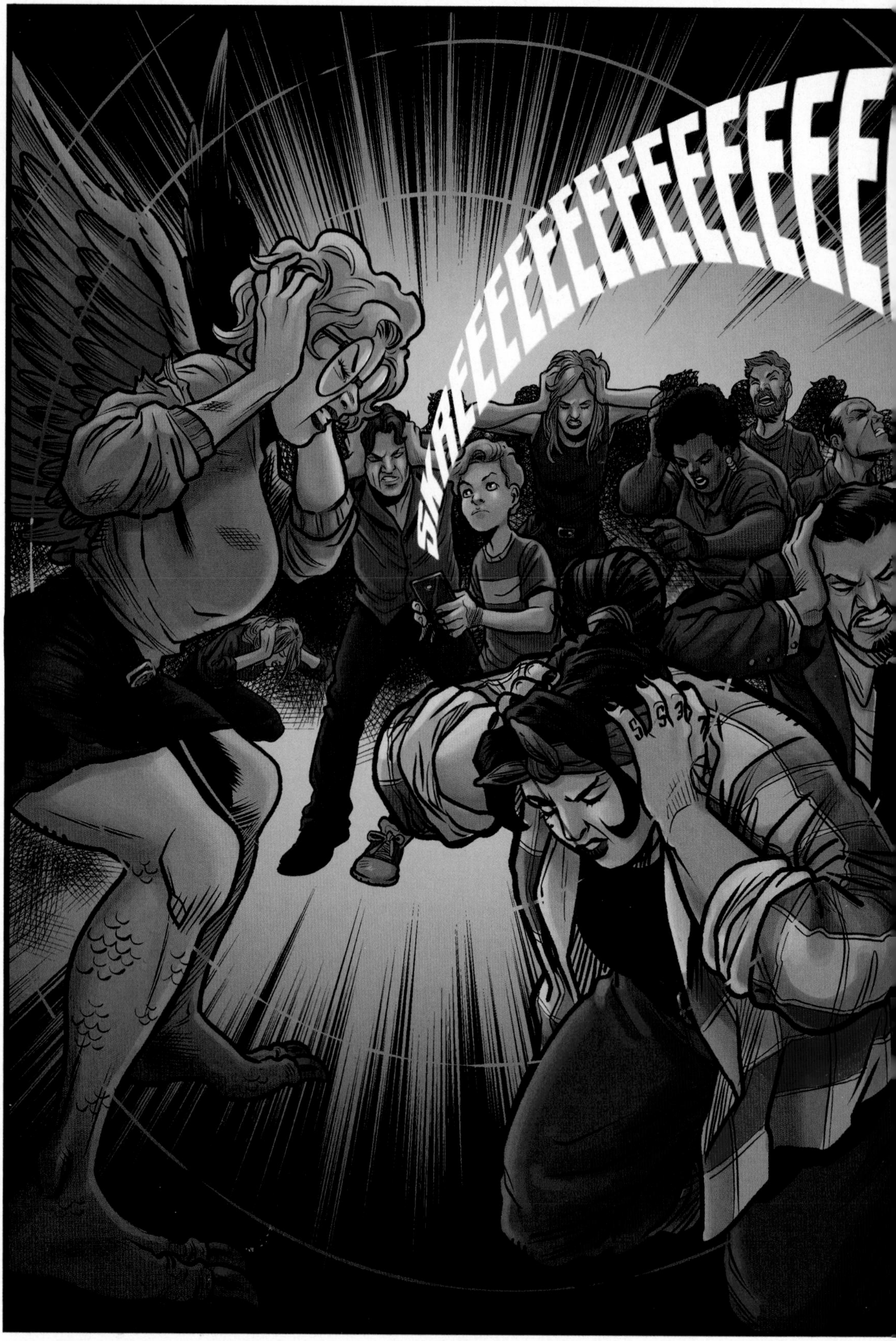
SKREEEEEEEEEEEEEEEEE

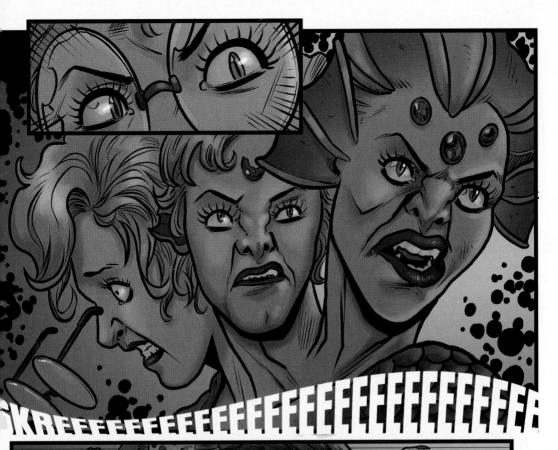

SKREEEEEEEEEEEEEEEEEEEEEEEEEEEEE

RRRREEEEEEEEEEEEEEEEEEEEEEEEEEEEE

RRREEEEEEEEEEEEEEEEEEE---

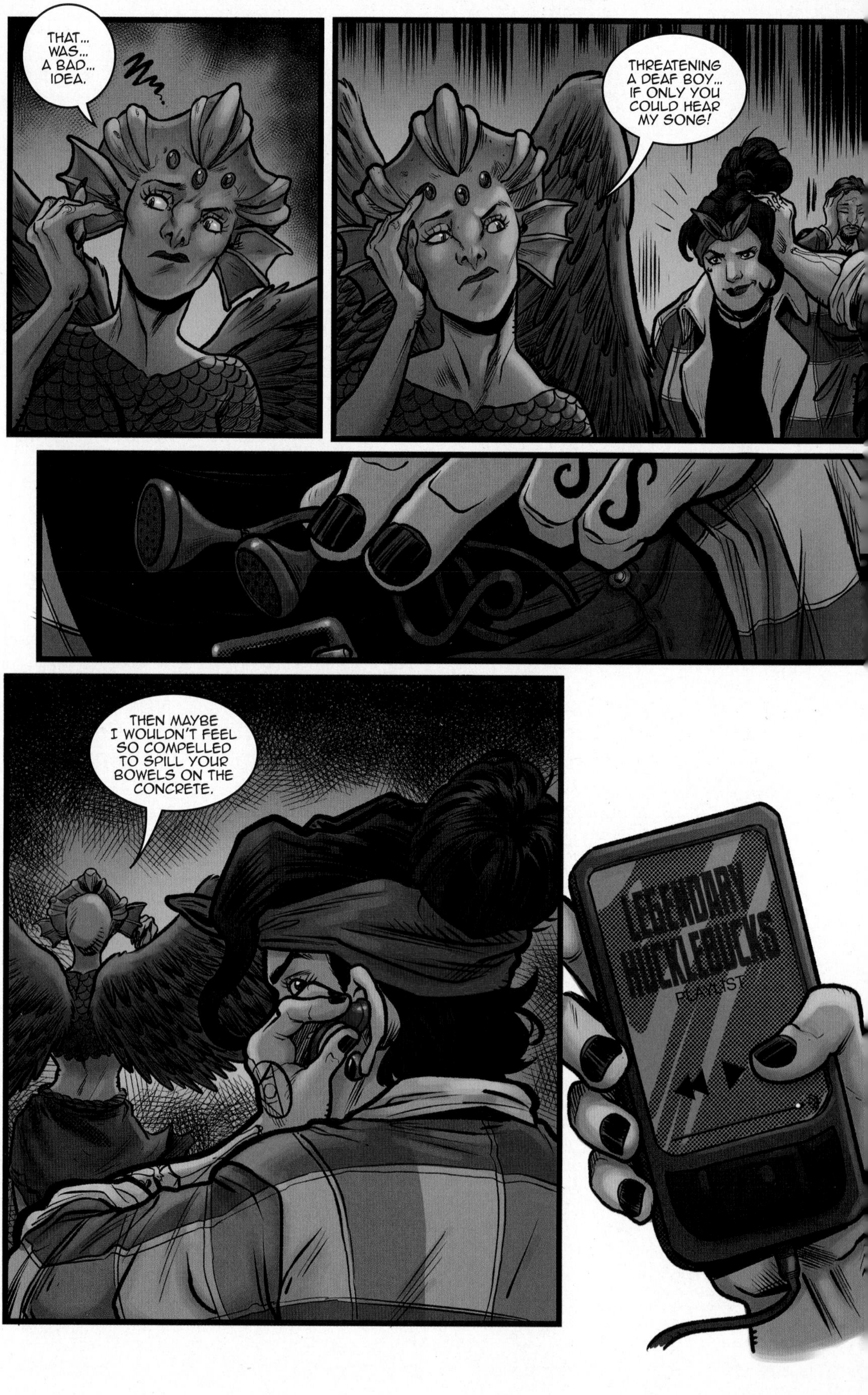
THAT... WAS... A BAD... IDEA.
THREATENING A DEAF BOY... IF ONLY YOU COULD HEAR MY SONG!
THEN MAYBE I WOULDN'T FEEL SO COMPELLED TO SPILL YOUR BOWELS ON THE CONCRETE.
LEGENDARY HUCKLEBUCKS
PLAYLIST

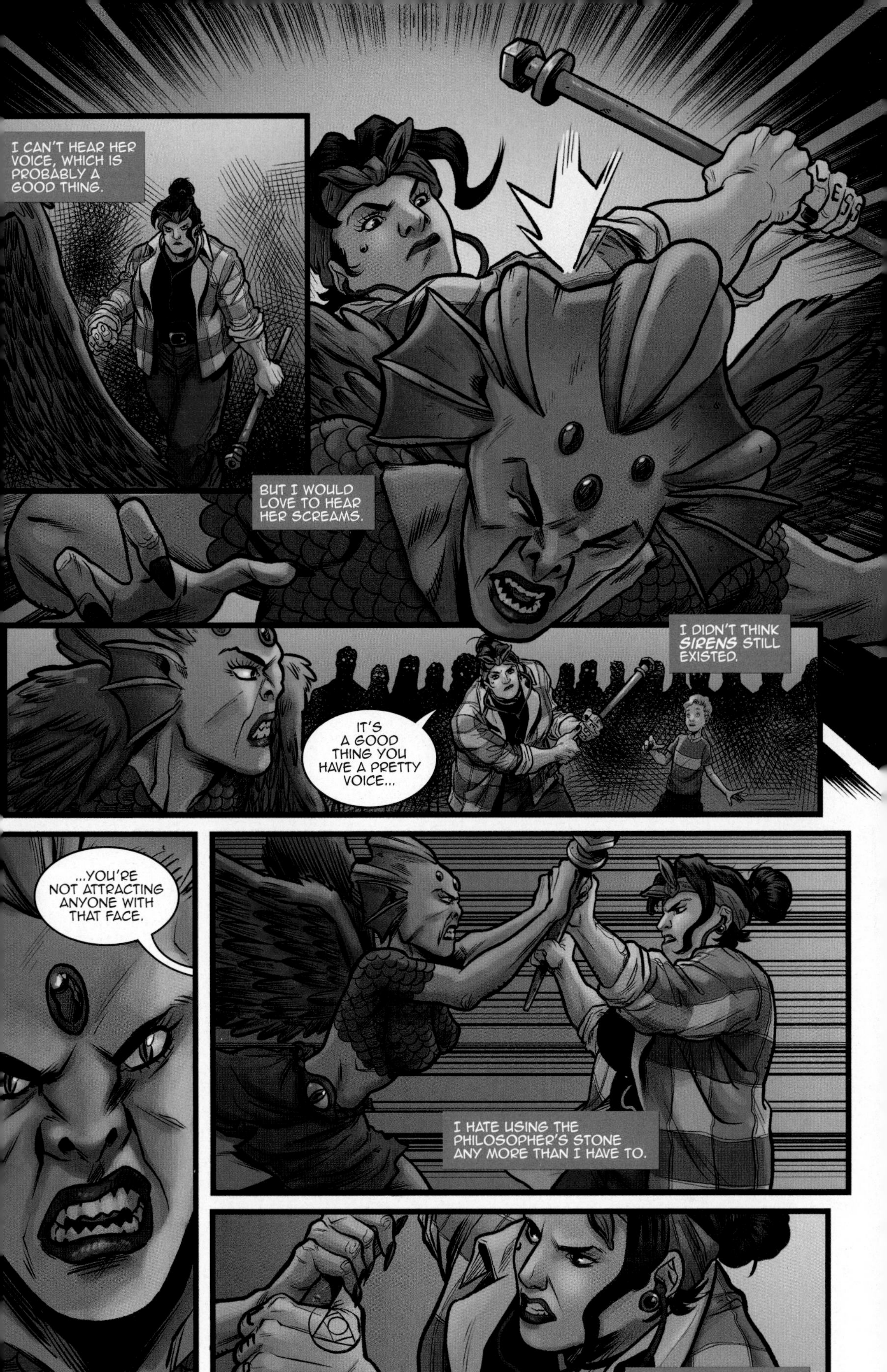
I CAN'T HEAR HER VOICE, WHICH IS PROBABLY A GOOD THING.
BUT I WOULD LOVE TO HEAR HER SCREAMS.
I DIDN'T THINK SIRENS STILL EXISTED.
IT'S A GOOD THING YOU HAVE A PRETTY VOICE...
...YOU'RE NOT ATTRACTING ANYONE WITH THAT FACE.
I HATE USING THE PHILOSOPHER'S STONE ANY MORE THAN I HAVE TO.
IT LEAVES ME FEELING... OFF SOMEHOW.

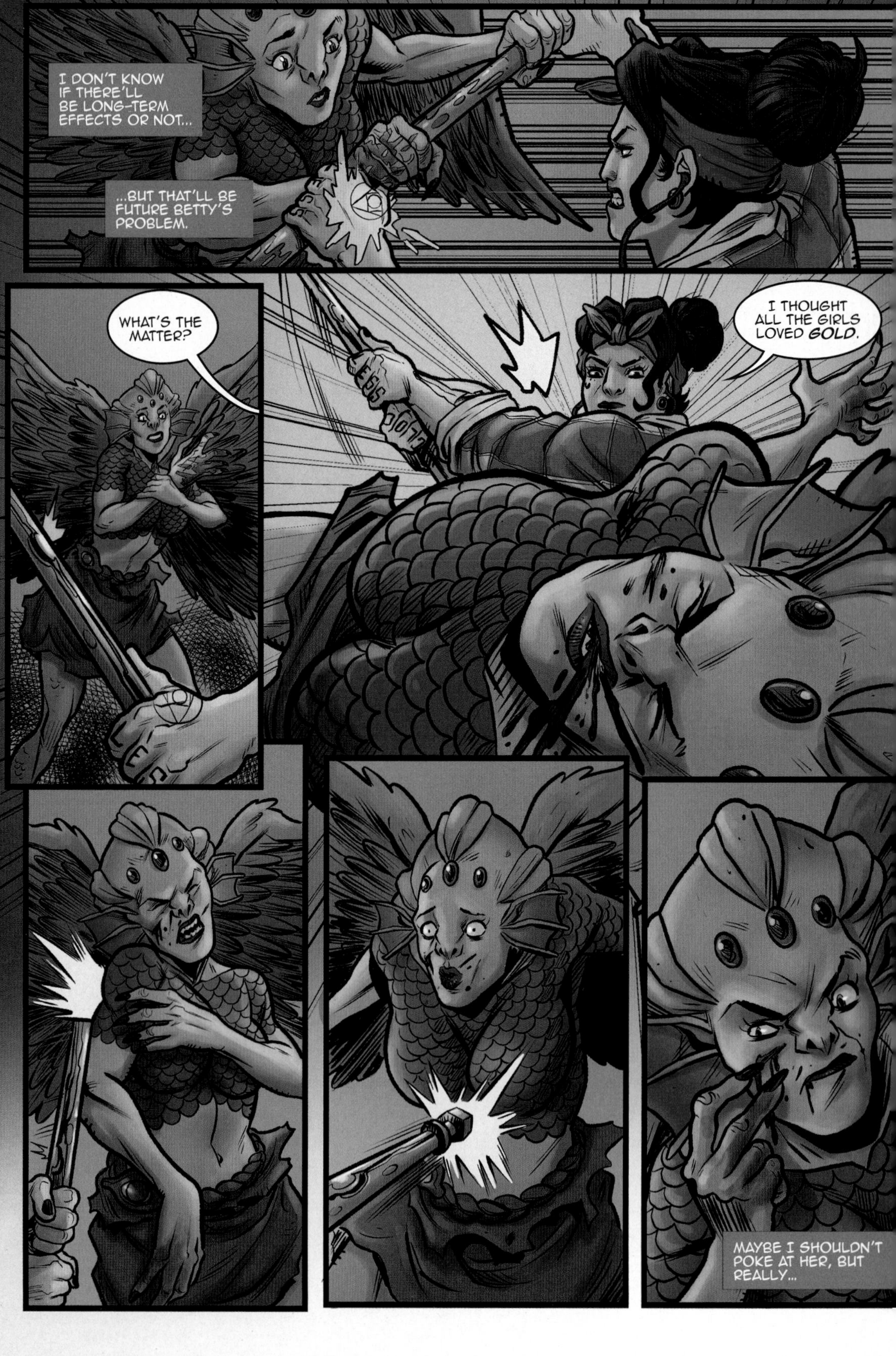
I DON'T KNOW IF THERE'LL BE LONG-TERM EFFECTS OR NOT...
...BUT THAT'LL BE FUTURE BETTY'S PROBLEM.
WHAT'S THE MATTER?
I THOUGHT ALL THE GIRLS LOVED GOLD.
MAYBE I SHOULDN'T POKE AT HER, BUT REALLY...

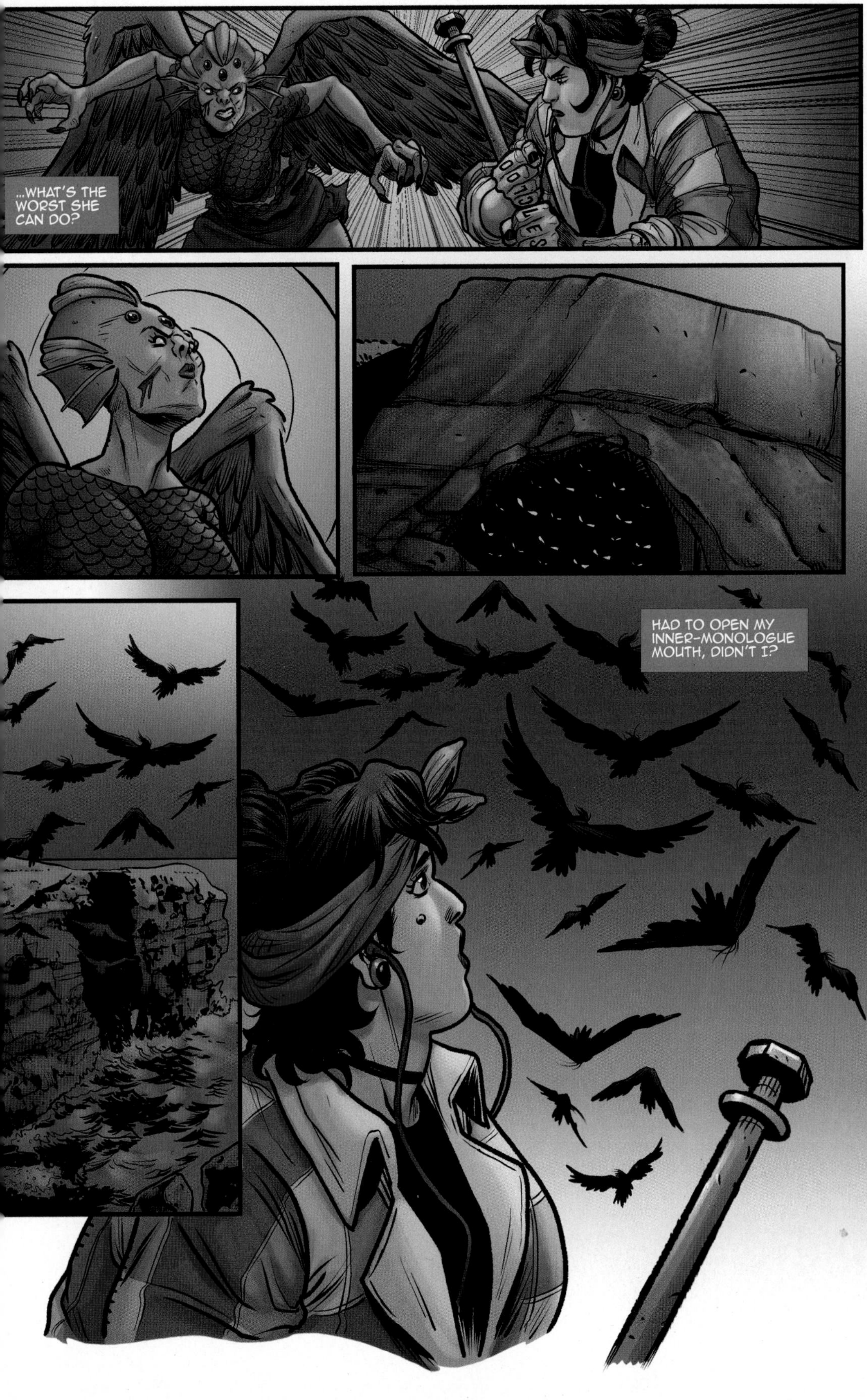
...WHAT'S THE WORST SHE CAN DO?
HAD TO OPEN MY INNER-MONOLOGUE MOUTH, DIDN'T I?

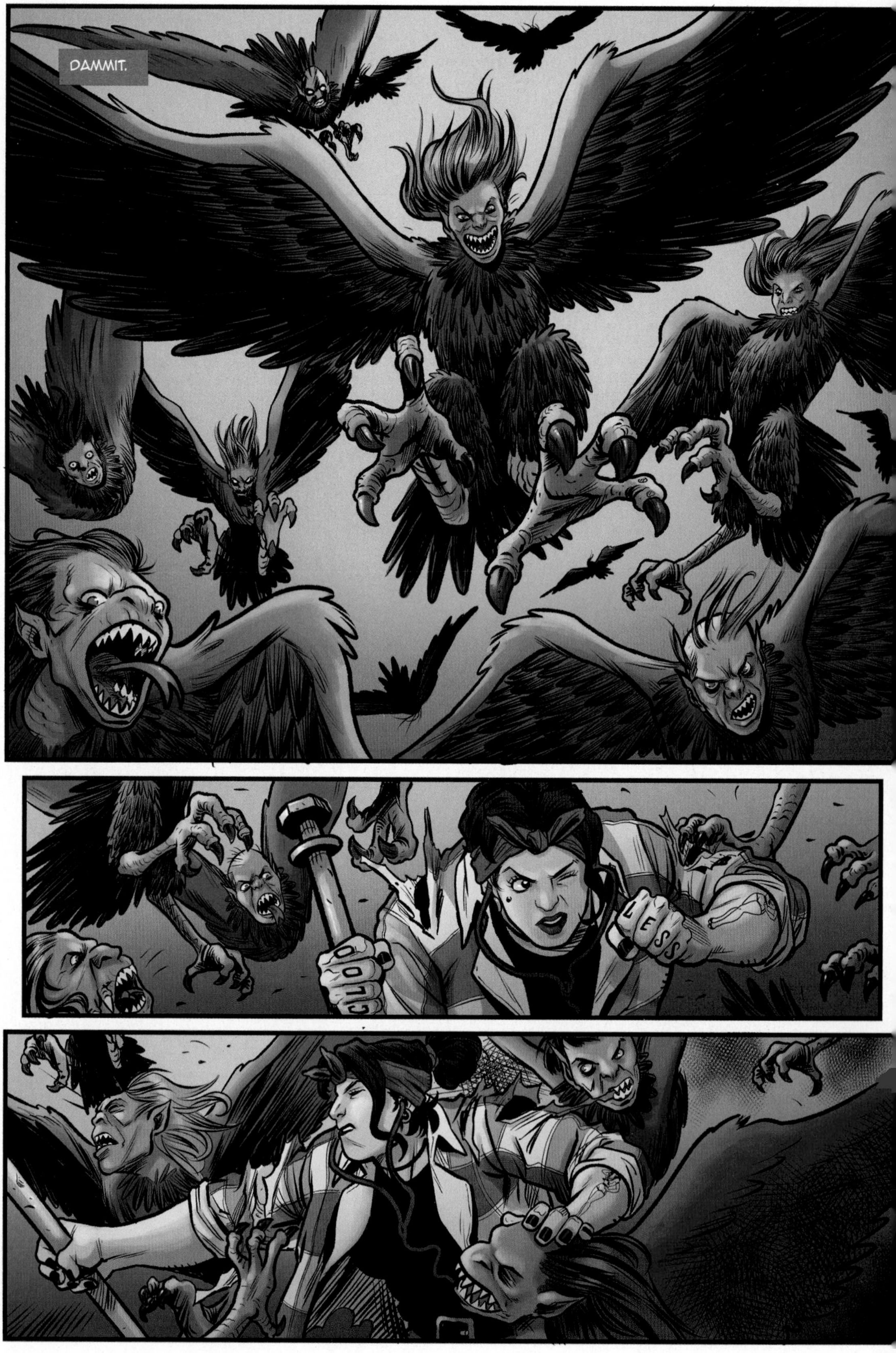
DAMMIT.
LESS

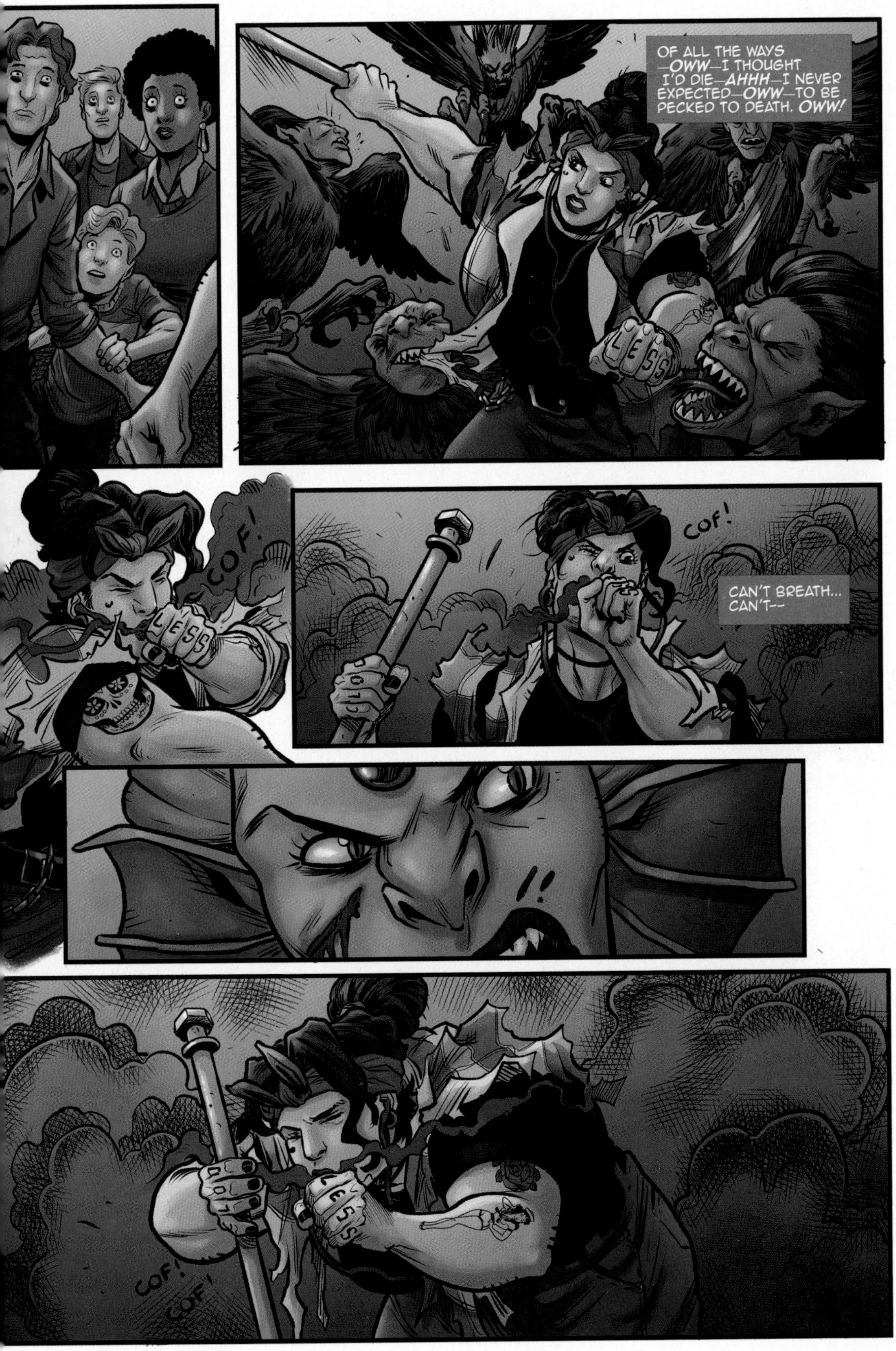

OF ALL THE WAYS —OWW—I THOUGHT I'D DIE—AHHH—I NEVER EXPECTED—OWW—TO BE PECKED TO DEATH. OWW!
COF!
COF!
CAN'T BREATH... CAN'T--
!!
COF!
COF!

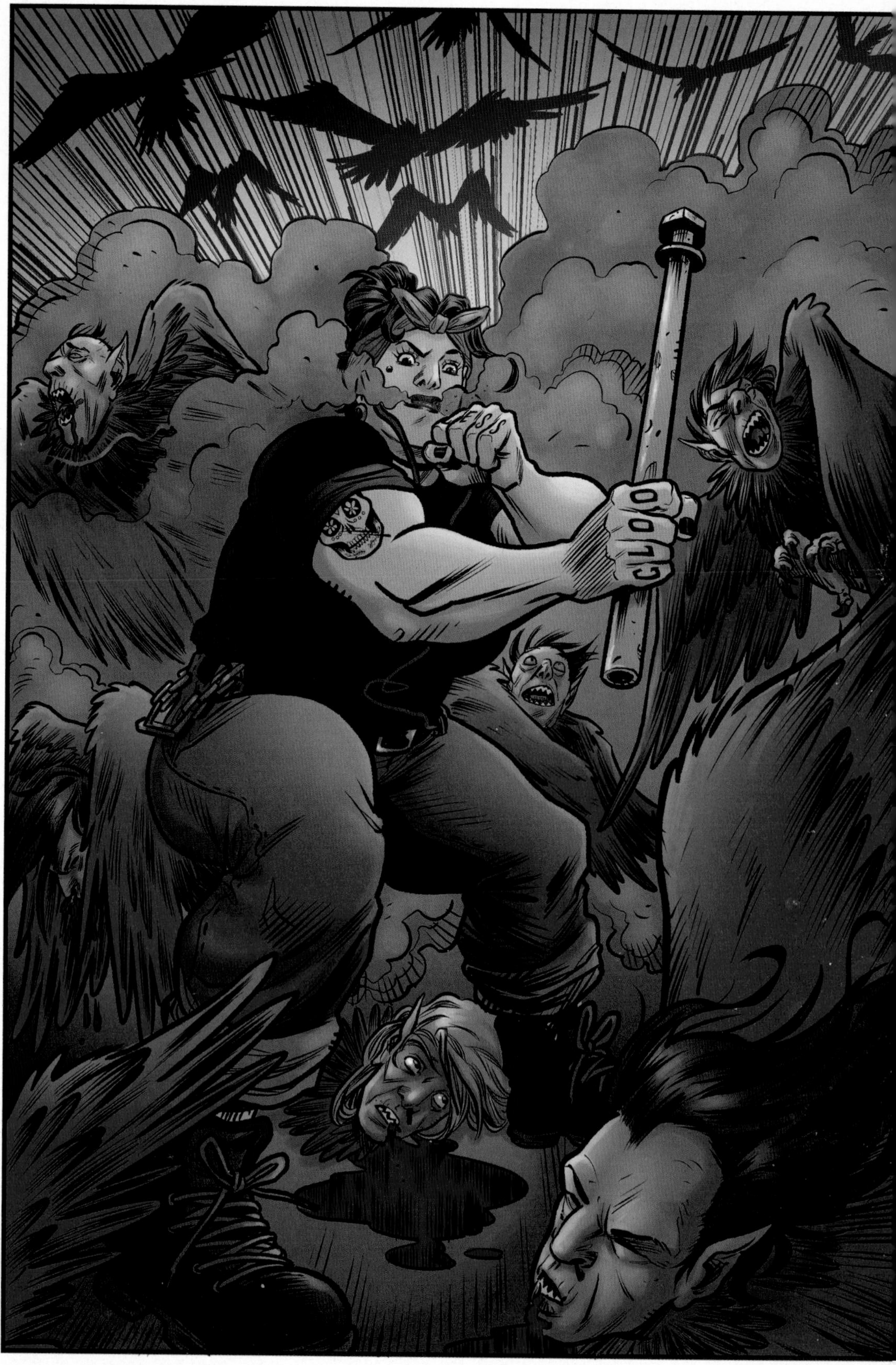

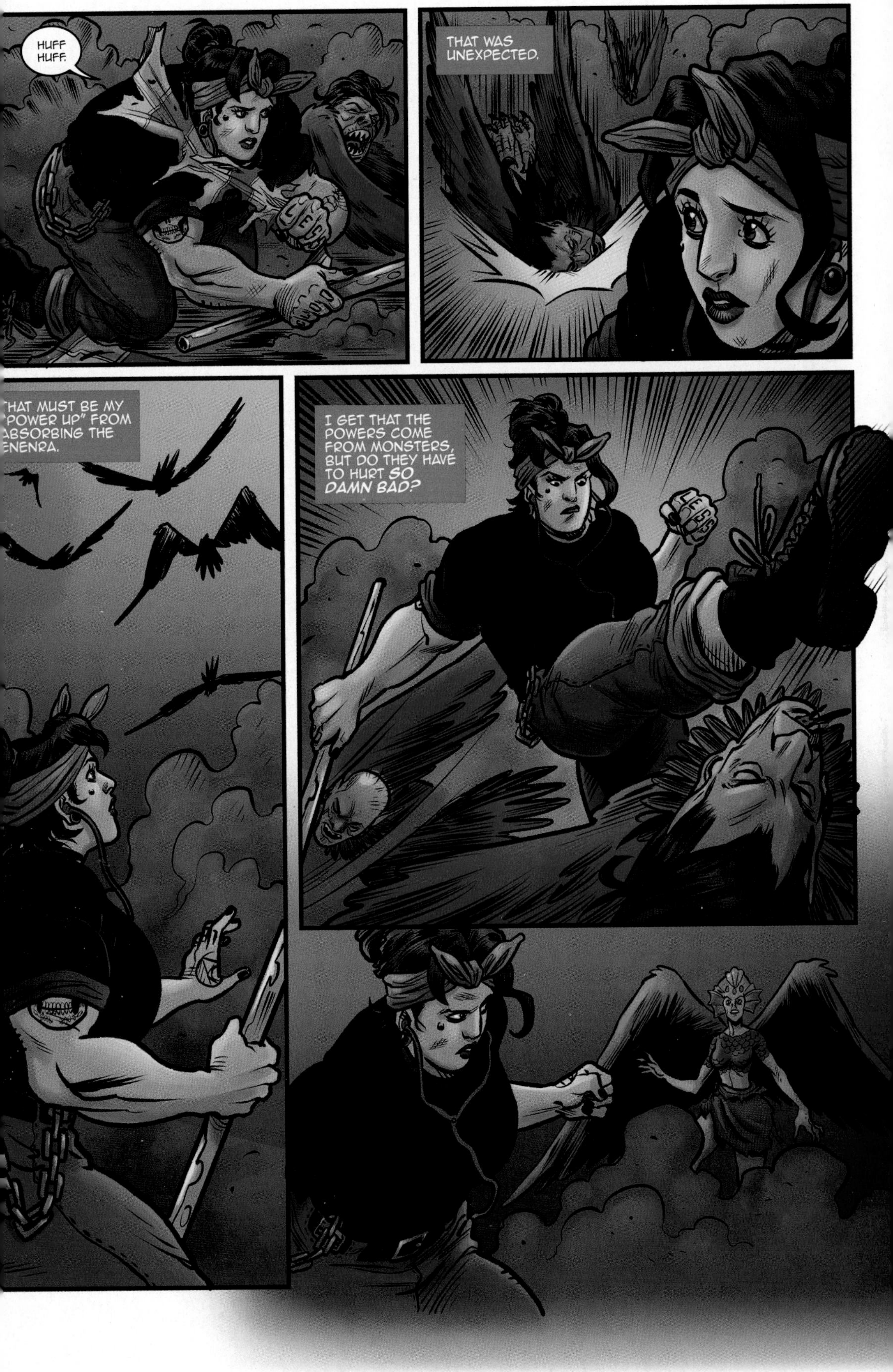
HUFF HUFF.
THAT WAS UNEXPECTED.
HAT MUST BE MY "POWER UP" FROM ABSORBING THE ENENRA.
I GET THAT THE POWERS COME FROM MONSTERS, BUT DO THEY HAVE TO HURT SO DAMN BAD?

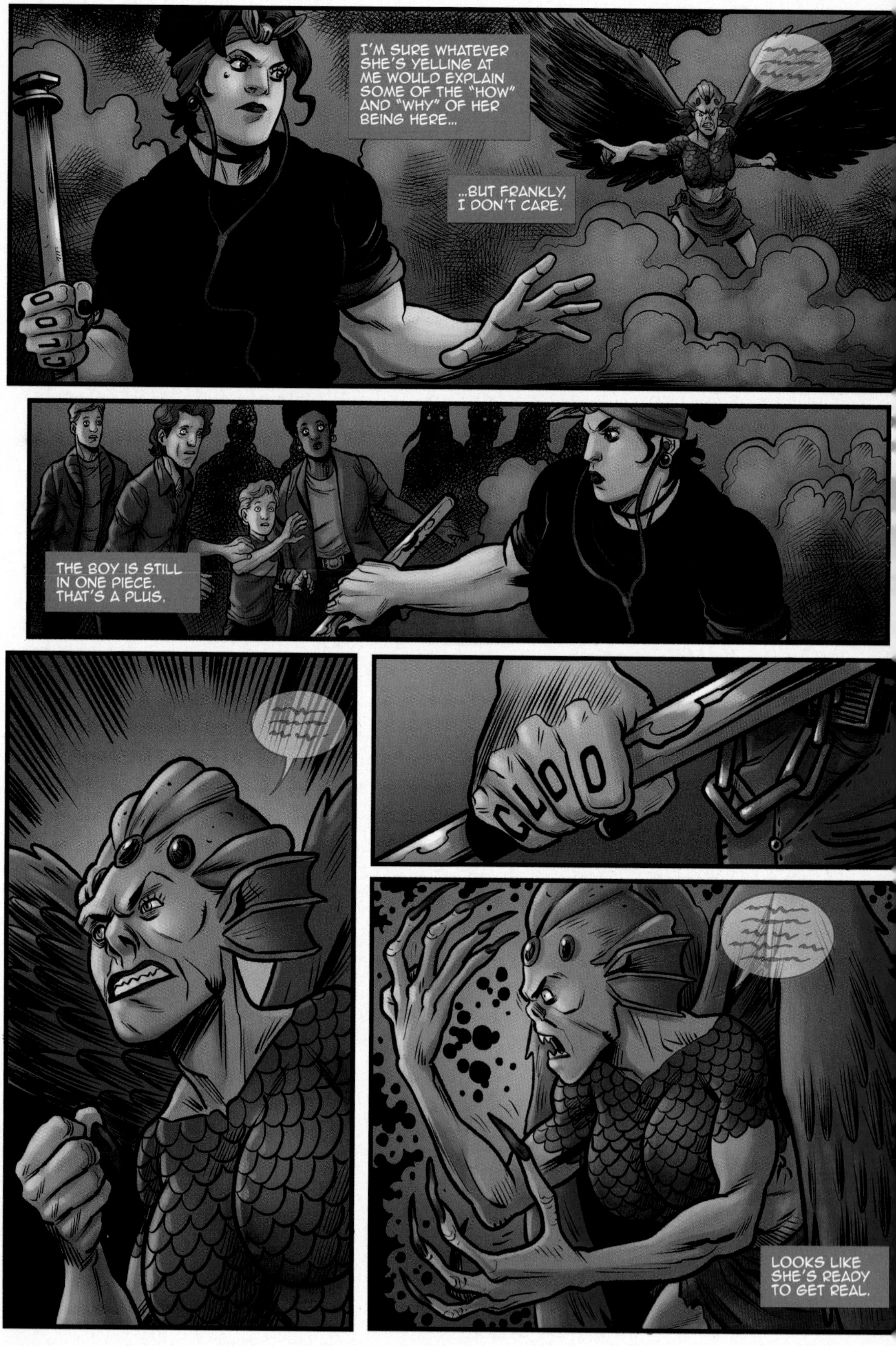
I'M SURE WHATEVER SHE'S YELLING AT ME WOULD EXPLAIN SOME OF THE "HOW" AND "WHY" OF HER BEING HERE...
...BUT FRANKLY, I DON'T CARE.
THE BOY IS STILL IN ONE PIECE. THAT'S A PLUS.
LOOKS LIKE SHE'S READY TO GET REAL.

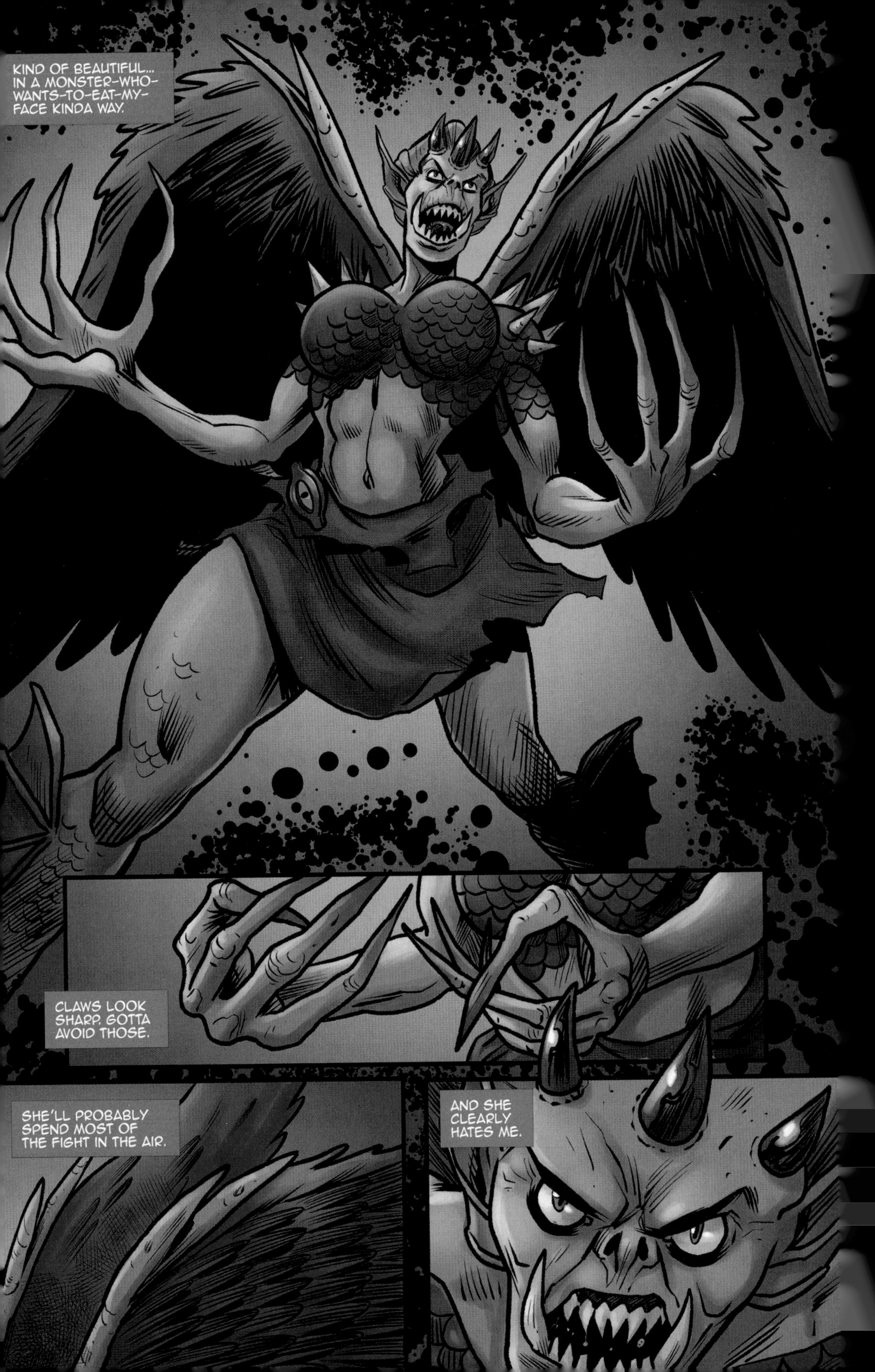
KIND OF BEAUTIFUL... IN A MONSTER-WHO-WANTS-TO-EAT-MY-FACE KINDA WAY.
CLAWS LOOK SHARP. GOTTA AVOID THOSE.
SHE'LL PROBABLY SPEND MOST OF THE FIGHT IN THE AIR.
AND SHE CLEARLY HATES ME.

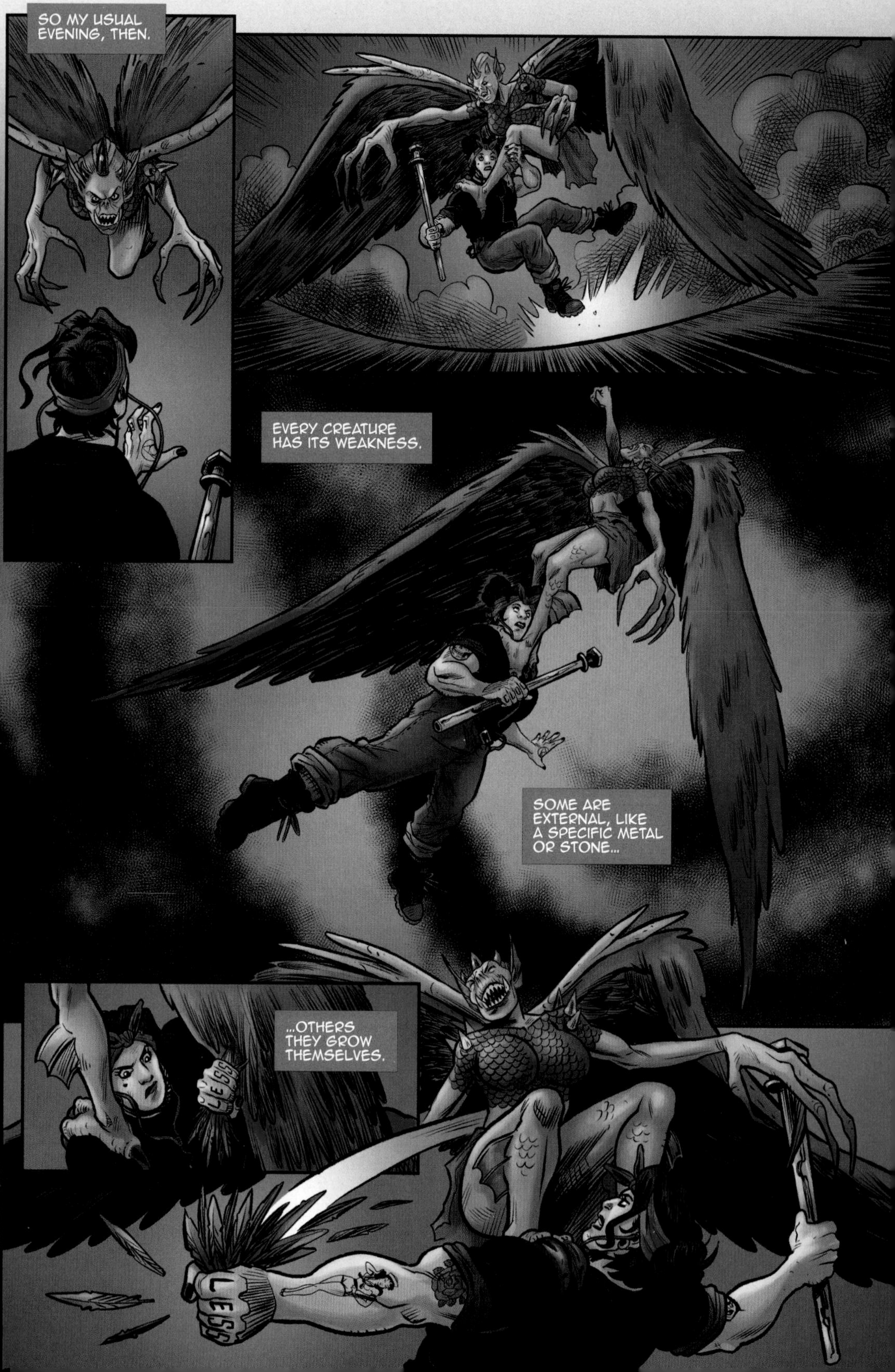
SO MY USUAL EVENING, THEN.
EVERY CREATURE HAS ITS WEAKNESS.
SOME ARE EXTERNAL, LIKE A SPECIFIC METAL OR STONE...
...OTHERS THEY GROW THEMSELVES.

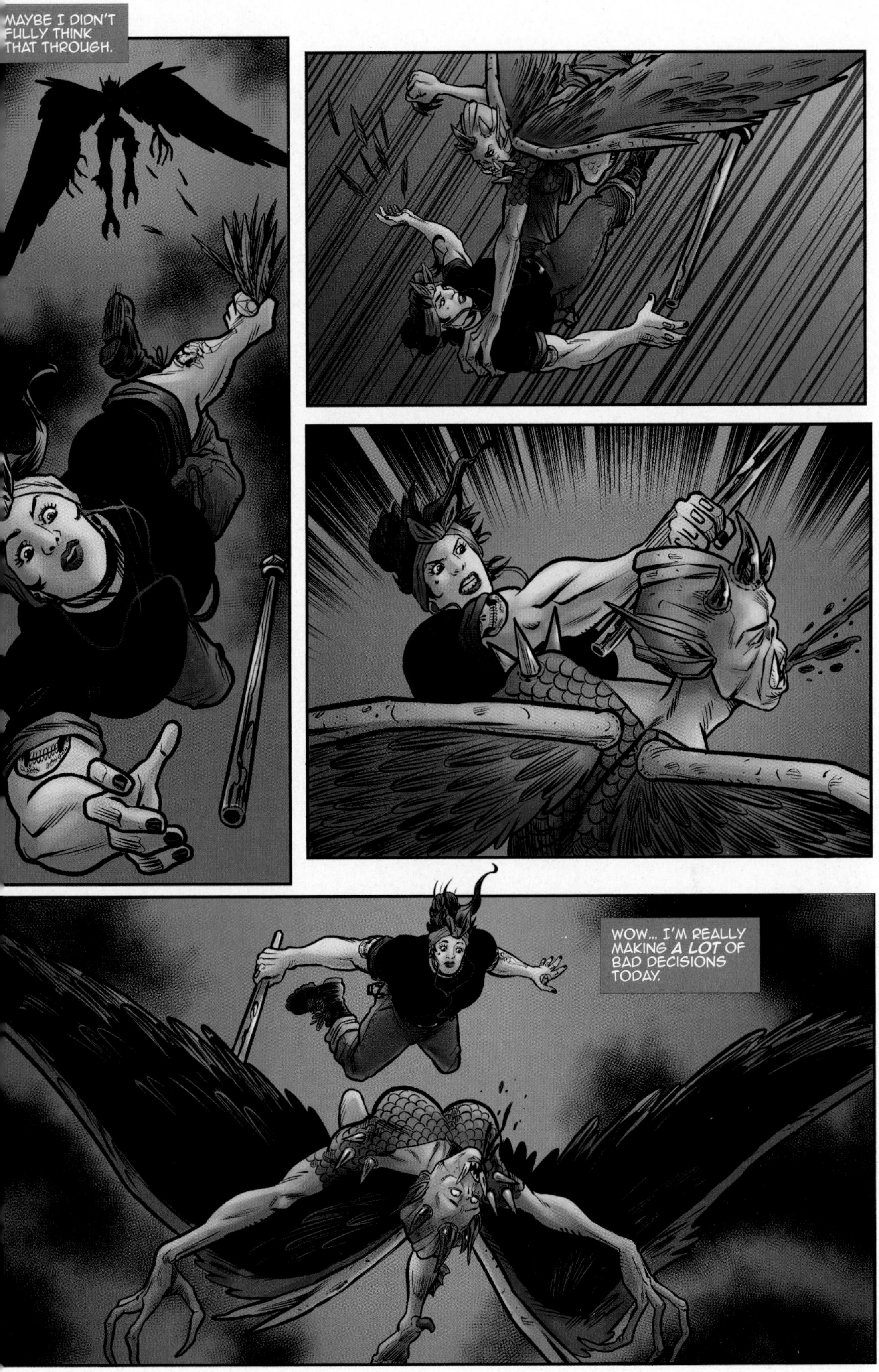
MAYBE I DIDN'T FULLY THINK THAT THROUGH.
WOW... I'M REALLY MAKING *A LOT* OF BAD DECISIONS TODAY.

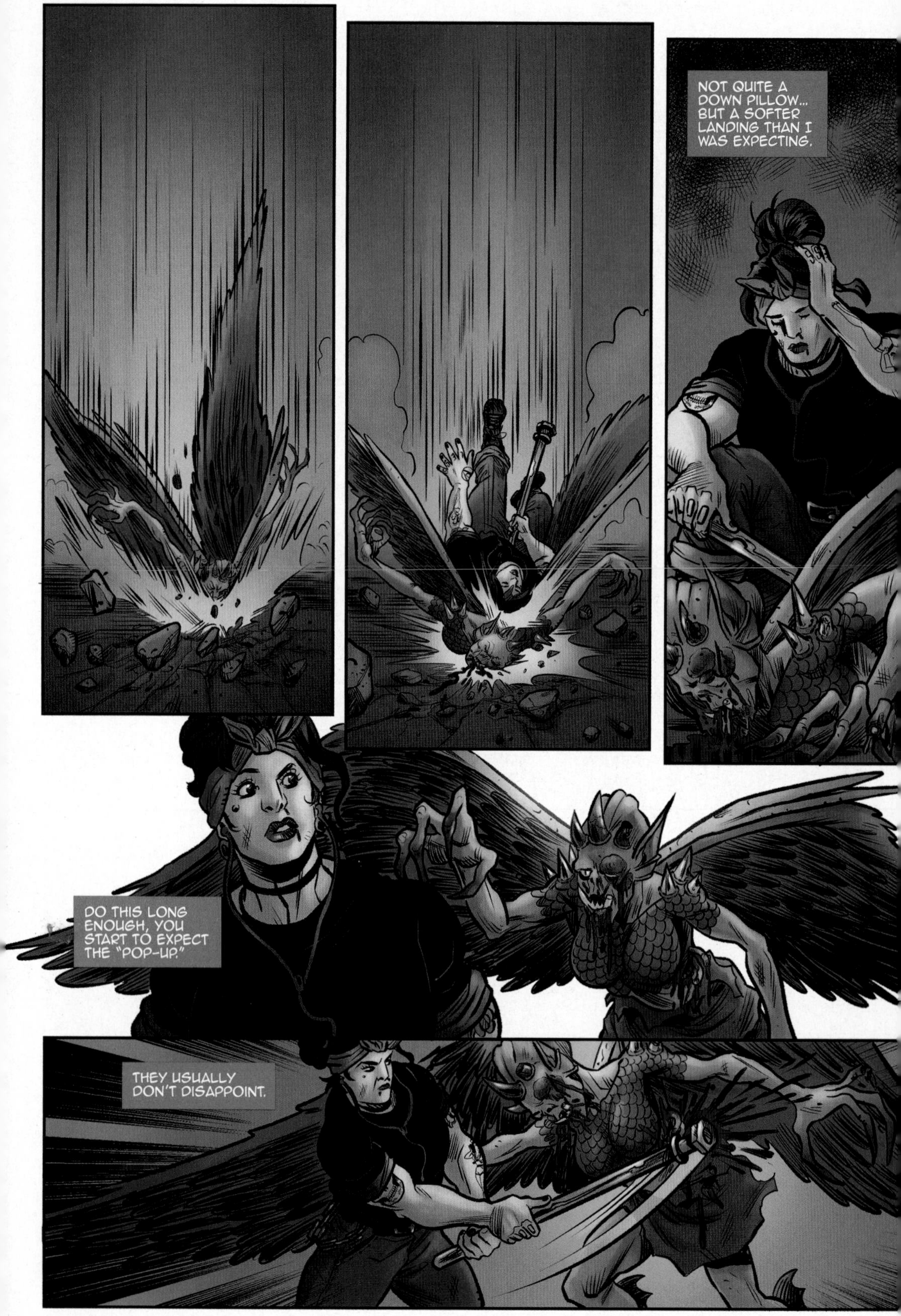
NOT QUITE A DOWN PILLOW... BUT A SOFTER LANDING THAN I WAS EXPECTING.
DO THIS LONG ENOUGH, YOU START TO EXPECT THE "POP-UP."
THEY USUALLY DON'T DISAPPOINT.

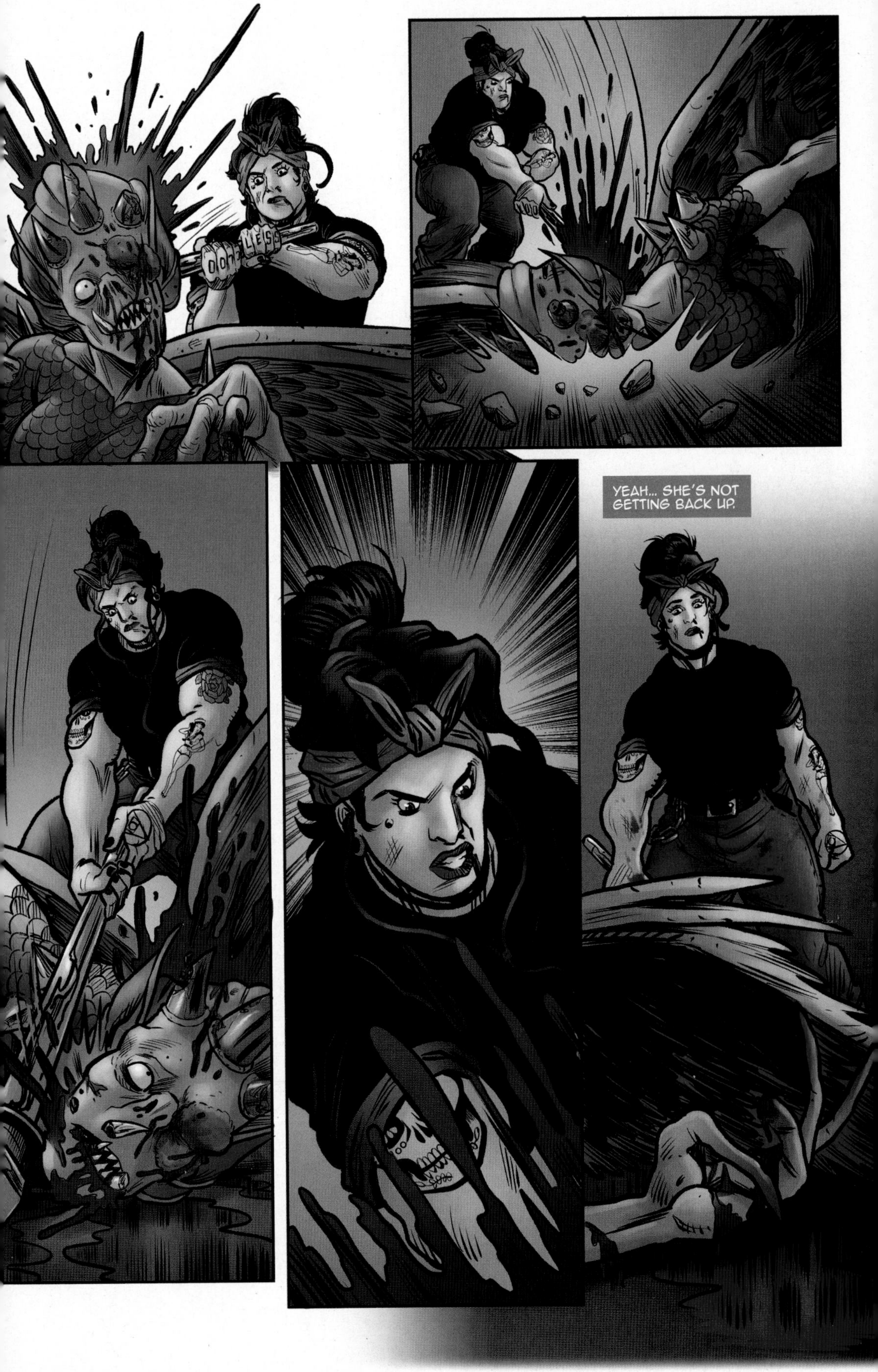
YEAH... SHE'S NOT GETTING BACK UP.

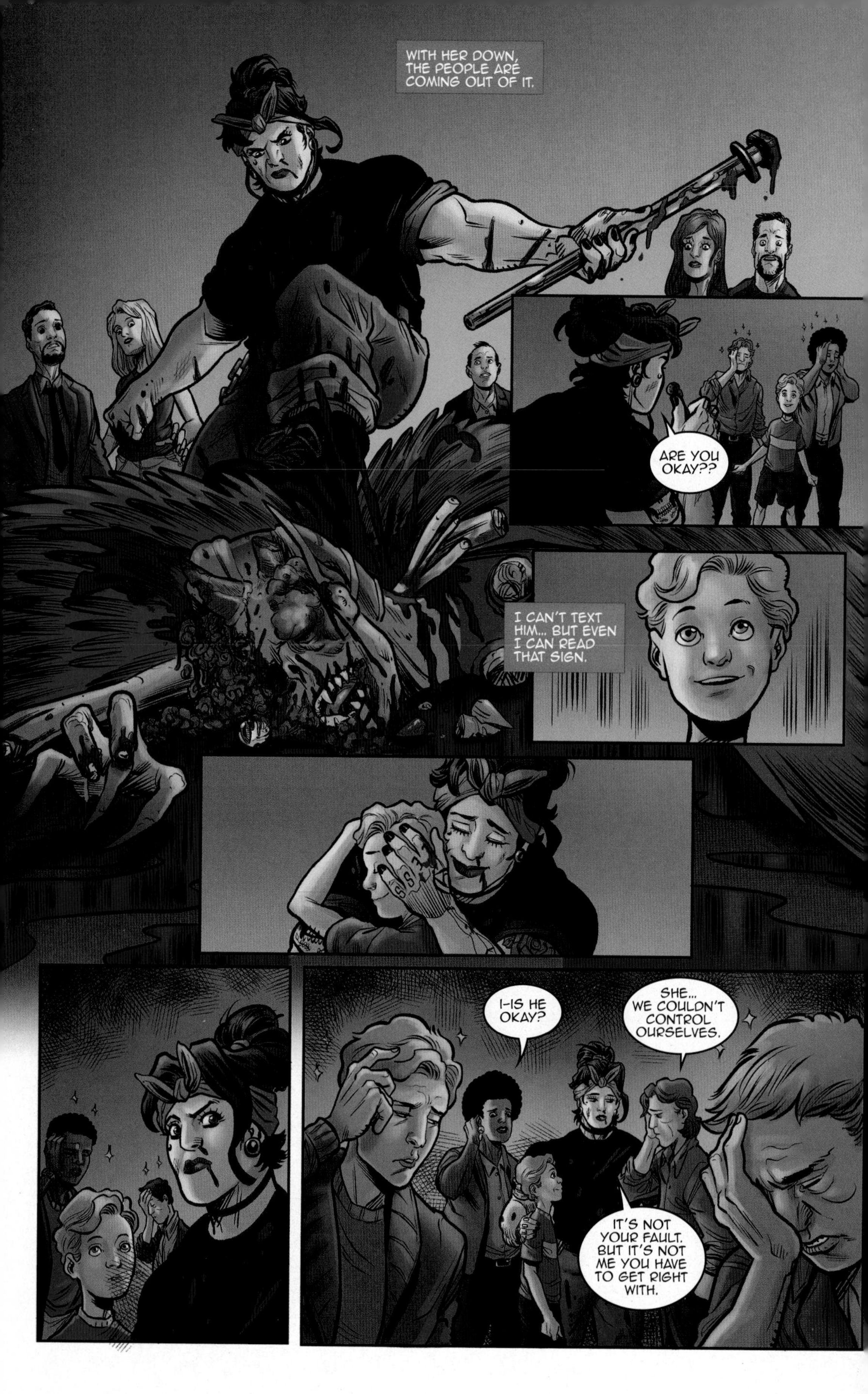
WITH HER DOWN, THE PEOPLE ARE COMING OUT OF IT.
ARE YOU OKAY??
I CAN'T TEXT HIM... BUT EVEN I CAN READ THAT SIGN.
I-IS HE OKAY?
SHE... WE COULDN'T CONTROL OURSELVES.
IT'S NOT YOUR FAULT. BUT IT'S NOT ME YOU HAVE TO GET RIGHT WITH.

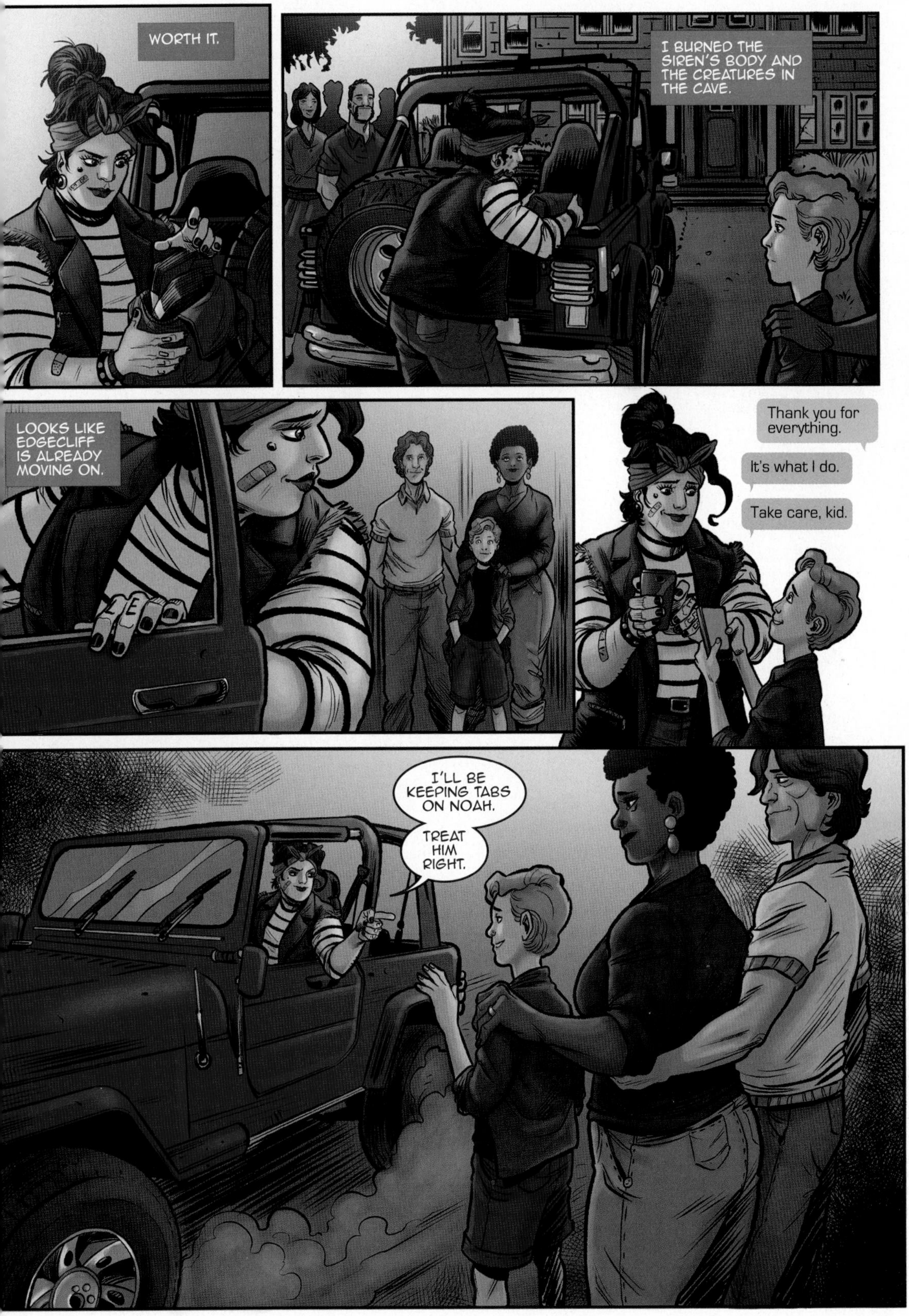
WORTH IT.
I BURNED THE SIREN'S BODY AND THE CREATURES IN THE CAVE.
LOOKS LIKE EDGECLIFF IS ALREADY MOVING ON.
Thank you for everything.
It's what I do.
Take care, kid.
I'LL BE KEEPING TABS ON NOAH.
TREAT HIM RIGHT.

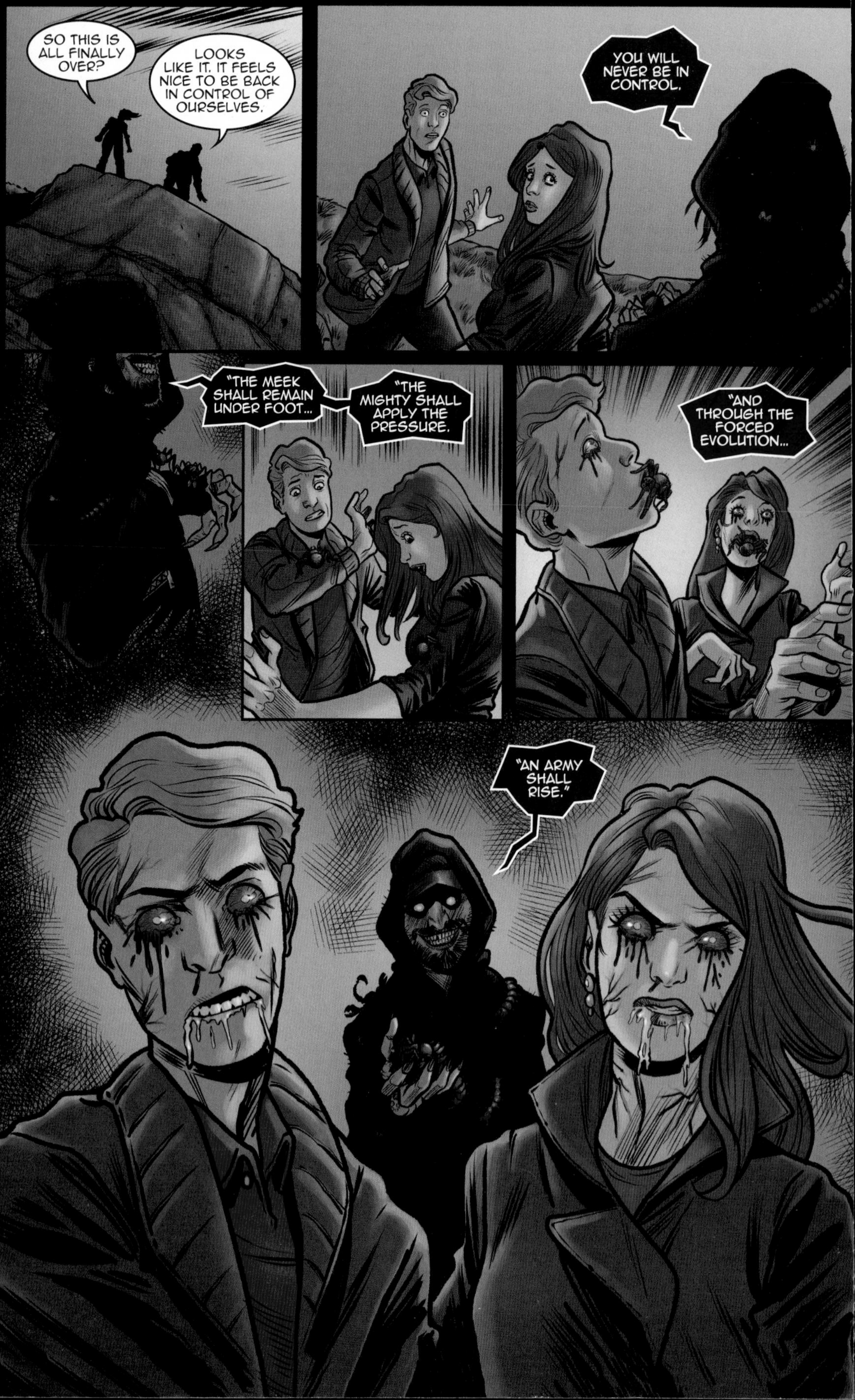
SO THIS IS ALL FINALLY OVER?
LOOKS LIKE IT. IT FEELS NICE TO BE BACK IN CONTROL OF OURSELVES.
YOU WILL NEVER BE IN CONTROL.
"THE MEEK SHALL REMAIN UNDER FOOT...
"THE MIGHTY SHALL APPLY THE PRESSURE.
"AND THROUGH THE FORCED EVOLUTION...
"AN ARMY SHALL RISE."